FRUIT FOR THE
SPIRIT,
MEAT FOR THE
GRILL

RANDY TRAEGER

Fruit for the Spirit, Meat for the Grill
© 2016 Randy Traeger

Published by
Deep River Books
Sisters, Oregon
www.deepriverbooks.com

ISBN: 9781940269863

Library of Congress: 2016939512

Cover design by Jason Enterline

Published in the United States

CONTENTS

PREFACE

As a child I often felt driven not only to succeed, but also to be noticed by my parents and peers. I wanted others to see me as good enough, worthy, and outstanding. As I grew older, these desires didn't disappear; they only grew stronger.

Through grade school, high school, and college, I remained passionately driven to achieve, taking on more and more, always proud of my good deeds. At one point, I had taken on so many good things that, like that camel loaded with sticks, my back began to sway under the pressure.

Vice and evil are worthy adversaries. They looked at me and said, "This Randy Traeger guy is a good man, how are we going to take him down? Let's load him up with so many good things that he cracks under the pressure." That is exactly what happened.

From the mid-1980s to the mid-1990s, I had taken on the tasks of being a husband and father of seven, president of the parish council, vice-president of sales and marketing for our $25 million barbecue grill manufacturing business, assistant fire chief, EMT and ambulance driver, manager of a restaurant LLC, mayor of the town where I lived, and assistant high school football coach. I started to sway under the weight. My life was completely out of balance.

Then, on September 14, 2012, I contracted a rare bone infection in my pelvis. I was hospitalized and nearly didn't make it through the early fevers. Doctors installed a direct line to my heart to administer the antibiotics that pumped into me twenty-four hours a day. In January of the following year, following several blood transfusions, doctors determined that the antibiotics alone were not working and

I needed surgery. They operated on February 5, 2013, and resumed the antibiotics.

Until this time, I had rarely been sick a day in my life. I took the whole episode as God telling me that I had better slow down and pay more attention to Him. He had put me on my knees to get my attention with this bone infection.

While recovering from the surgery, I decided that I would give more back to God. I started to work harder on a concept I had formulated back in 2000 for a ministry called Virtue First. Its mission would be to promote virtue and help rebuild the character of America.

After coaching high school football for more than two decades, I had come to the conclusion that it really wasn't about winning and losing. It was about establishing positive relationships with kids and equipping them with philosophies that will grow them into better husbands, friends, dads, and men.

I poured what I thought was everything I had into this venture, but I was wrong. I still fostered a strong sense of self-consciousness and self-focus. Neither of these two attributes would serve God on the mission He had in store for me.

So He decided to make me lie on the ground and take me all the way down to dust.

For health reasons we sold our businesses, but then came the stock market crash, and I lost just about everything. Some hedge fund investments then went south. I couldn't find another job. We lost our health insurance and three homes. No job, no money, no home. Throughout this period, I felt compelled to continue funding the nonprofit I had started to help kids.

I was under more stress during this period than at any other time in my life. But the camel's back finally gave way, and I broke under the stress. In the early morning hours of December 8, 2014, my wife and daughter found me in our kitchen talking to a light bulb. I was hallucinating. With the help of my father, they took me to the emergency room, and doctors learned that the ammonia levels in my brain had become toxic. They diagnosed me with hepatic encephalopathy caused by nonalcoholic cirrhosis of the liver, which resulted from heredity, a fatty liver, and stress.

I was cooked.

Everything in my life needed to change. I was ready to turn my entire being over to God. I wanted God to control every area of my life. I wanted to serve with my whole being, not just most of it.

I became even more passionate for promoting virtue, especially to the lost and hurting and all people who suffer. I started to write more and expand the curriculums our nonprofit offers to serve those in need.

One of those areas of neediness is manhood.

Men need help and support nowadays. It is my hope that in some small way this book provides advice that may be helpful to men in their relationships with others.

—Randy Traeger

INTRODUCTION

A recipe is a set of instructions or advice for preparing food. The English word *recipe* comes from the Latin imperative for "take" because recipes typically used to start, "Take one pound of flour . . . take a cup of butter." The modern recipe often follows this format: (1) a list of necessary food ingredients and sometimes special equipment; (2) the preparation needed to get the food ready to cook, and (3) the method, which spells out the cooking procedures to achieve the finished dish. A recipe can also include explanatory notes, which might give advice about ingredients, including possible substitutions, tips on method, snippets of historical and cultural background, and an acknowledgment of the recipe's source.

This book contains a collection of a variety of barbecue grilling recipes. These recipes were designed to work best on a Traeger grill. But many of them can be cooked on whatever type of grill you own.

The book also contains what I call relational manhood recipes for men who are fathers, brothers, teammates, coworkers, husbands, sons, and friends. Why include such "recipes"?

The men in our country (young and old alike) are currently experiencing a crisis of masculinity. The meaning of manhood has been perverted by our culture. In earlier times, fathers and their sons often worked together. The father worked on the farm and his sons worked with him. Or the father taught his sons a trade. Most boys observed male behavior every day and built their ideas of masculinity from the men around them. With the industrial revolution, when men went to work in factories and boys went to school, fathers and sons were together less often, usually after a hard working day when both were tired. Boys were exposed to only limited aspects of masculinity. Many "rites of passage" have gradually disappeared as verbal history and stories about men have faded.

Today the separation of fathers from their sons is possibly even more pervasive. Men are largely confined to factories and offices while boys are at school for longer and longer periods. Meanwhile, the home is largely the woman's preserve. With fathers physically and emotionally separated from their sons, it's hard for boys to learn what it means to be male. But in our society boys learn about masculinity one way or another. Unfortunately, most of those other ways provide a limited and distorted picture of masculinity and not the comprehensive picture provided by a father.

At present, there are four obvious ways for boys to learn about masculinity:

- From their fathers or another male role model;
- From the media, which often tells boys that there are three types of men—competitive sportsmen, violent men, and clowns;
- From their peers, among whom it is frequently the most aggressive and violent male who calls the shots and ends up providing an example of "successful" masculinity;
- By "default," when boys are mostly surrounded by women at home and school and they begin to develop anti-female attitudes in which anything associated with women—like showing emotions, caring for others, looking after your body, talking about feelings and, critical to boys' education, being literate and good in school—is degraded and to be avoided at all cost.

Other than the first and preferred method of a boy learning about masculinity from his own father or a close role model, the other ways of learning masculinity convey a limited, stereotyped, and distorted picture of macho masculinity.

Boys should learn masculinity from the men with whom they spend time and have good relationships. Their fathers, uncles, grandfathers, step-fathers, older brothers, coaches, youth pastors, teachers, and neighbors can all help boys develop a healthy picture of maleness. Masculinity is best taught through relationships with men who model responsibility, courageous leadership, acting for justice on behalf of others, and empathy.

The way to solve our culture's crisis of masculinity is to devote ourselves to spending time with young men and talking to them about what it means to be a man. I hope that this book will be a useful guide to help every man do just that.

1

FATHERS

A good father makes all the difference in a kid's life. He's a pillar of strength, support, and discipline. His work is endless and oftentimes thankless. But in the end, it shows in the sound, well-adjusted children he raises. The manly characteristics of a father include:

- He's a good disciplinarian. A good father loves his children, but he doesn't let them get away with murder. He strongly disapproves of the trouble his kids get into, but he uses tough love to correct. He does this through the power of his words, not his fists. Likewise, a father doesn't reward his children for actions that are expected of them, such as helping with house chores or performing well in school. If his child drops out of school, the father demands that he provide for himself, considering the child no longer wants to invest in his own future.

- He allows his kids to make some mistakes. A good father realizes that his children are human, and that making mistakes is part of growing up. Spending money recklessly, getting into minor car accidents, getting drunk and sick for the first time, even dating questionable girls are rites of passage, and a good father recognizes this. However, he makes it clear that repeated irresponsibility won't be tolerated.

- He's open minded. A good father understands that times, people, and tastes change over the years, and he doesn't try to maintain some gold standard of his own time. For example, he realizes that body piercings are commonplace, that tattoos are in style, and that people talk more candidly about personal issues. In other words, he allows his children to be citizens of their day and age.

- He teaches his children to appreciate things. A good father never lets his children take what they have for granted. From the food on the table to the good education he's paying for, a good father will make his children see the value in everything they have. He'll ask his child to get a job to help pay for a part of his first car, and take the time to illustrate how important a good education is. He doesn't let his kids treat him like an ATM.

- He accepts that his kids aren't exactly like him. Everyone is different, and a father knows this well. He won't expect his kids to live the same kind of life he does, and do the same kind of work. He also respects their values and opinions, as long as they don't harm the family or anyone else.

- He spends a large quantity of quality time with his children. A dad knows how to have fun with his kids by taking them to games and movies. He supports their sports teams by attending their events. He takes the time to listen to his kids and have a good, easy chat with them. He also makes time to help them with their homework, every night if necessary.

- He leads by example. A good father is above the old "do as I say, not as I do" credo. He will not smoke if he doesn't want his kids to do it, and he won't drink heavily. He teaches them to deal with conflict with a family member and with others by being firm but reasonable at the same time.

- A good father also illustrates the importance of affection by professing his love for their mother in front of them. He won't fight with her in their presence. In all, he adheres to the values he'd like his children to follow.

- A good father is also his children's public defender, standing up for them when needed. He waits for privacy to administer discipline. A safety net, a good father is also the person his kids turn to when things go wrong.

- He teaches his children lessons. A father figure is the prime source of knowledge in the ways of men, and teaches his kids accordingly. From shaving to being courageous, a father molds his kids into well-rounded members of society. He especially instructs them in proper etiquette, on being honest and keeping their word, and on being thankful.

- He protects his family at all costs. As the main provider of security and necessities, a father will do whatever he can for his family. He'll take a second job to provide for them, and he'll put his own safety on the line to keep them out of harm's way. This is how a father instills the importance of personal sacrifice in his children.

Manhood: Two Basic Ingredients

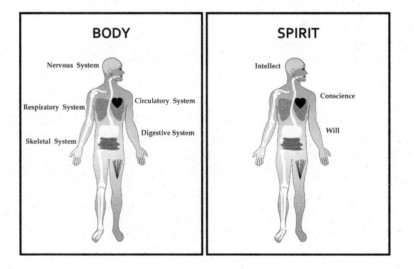

Every man is made of the two ingredients of body and spirit. While the man's body includes biological systems such as nervous, respiratory, skeletal, circulatory, digestive, and so on, another major ingredient is his spirit. We cannot see the spirit, but we know that the man has a spirit in the same way that we know electricity exists. Even though we can't see it directly, we see its effect when we turn on a light switch or the TV. In a similar way, we also know that the spirit exists because of its effects. The spirit's components are the intellect (the ability to learn and reason), the conscience (the inner sense of what is right or wrong in one's conduct or motives), and the will (the power to make decisions).

The physical health of the body is very important. Athletes are constantly striving to become bigger, stronger, and faster. They lift weights, have running and speed programs, and constantly practice specific skills to make their bodies as strong as possible. Athletes focus on maintaining a good diet. But the body is only part of the complete man.

Every man should ask himself what he is doing to strengthen his spirit.

Man's spirit is often overlooked, but to be strong it needs exercise and nourishment as much as the body does. If a man just exercises and nourishes his body and forgets to strengthen his spirit, his character will be uncoordinated, unbalanced, incomplete, and often misguided. For example, an athlete with all the physical talent in the world is no good to his team if, when facing adversity, he stops giving 100 percent, starts blaming other teammates, and subsequently is ejected from the game because he couldn't control his temper. This athlete needed to spend less time strengthening his body and more time strengthening his spirit.

Most American men need a character-development program for their spirits.

Cooking Time: Men Aged to Perfection

How long does it take to bake a man?

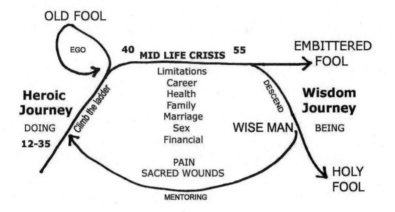

From the ages of about twelve to thirty-five, men generally work to climb the ladder of success. They complete their educations, pursue a career, and often start a family. They embark on a heroic journey toward their destiny. Between the ages of forty and fifty-five, most men face a crisis of limitations that the culture often calls a midlife crisis. This crisis is most often brought on by some painful experience—loss of a loved one, a broken marriage, career changes, job loss, a drug or alcohol addiction, death of a parent, the premature death of a child or friend, or a health problem. The coping skills the man used to overcome these things when he was younger simply don't work anymore. He has reached his limitations. He has climbed the ladder of success only to find that it was leaning against the wrong building (or no building at all). The man discovers that he has limitations, and he cannot be all things to all people.

Old Fools

Some men's egos make them immune to feeling the pain of their own limitations, and they continue blindly seeking more power, prestige, and possessions. These men are recognizable because they are often shallow, one-dimensional, materialistic people. They are "old fools," and you usually can find a lot of these guys on the golf course yelling at other golfers.

Embittered Fools

Some men take a second path where they feel the pain of their limitations, but they never come to terms with it. Rather than transform the pain with honesty and humility into "sacred wounds" of change, they transmit the pain to others. They continue to look for someone to blame. They remain negative, critical, and unhappy people. We call them "embittered fools." These are the grumpy old men.

Wise Men

If you leave the man in the oven to bake a little longer, many will eventually confront their own limitations and their own finality and embark on a wisdom journey. Men at this stage of the cooking process are called "wise men." These men have transformed their pain by surrendering. They have undergone a spiritual transformation and have stopped trying to ascend the ladder. They drop out of the rat race. They have entered a stage of "being" in which they care more about being and less about doing. They also learn to embrace others and listen to their stories. This wisdom journey often involves a period of time in the "wilderness," where the man passes through a dark place and emerges into the light on the other side. Wise men take what they have learned on their wisdom journeys and give it back by mentoring younger men. Wise men realize that it's not about *my* story (subjective, personal, worldly), nor is it about *our* story (traditions, community, country). Rather, it is about *the* story and a role greater than ourselves, our interdependence with others, our world, and God.

Holy Fools

Finally, if you leave the man in the oven too long, he will turn into a "holy fool." Holy fools are wise men who learn a lot on their wisdom journeys, but they internalize it all and never share it by mentoring younger men. These men are like recluse zen monks held up in some cave.

The development of a man involves a complicated cooking process in which extreme care must be used. Otherwise someone always gets burned.

Who Is Cooking for Our Kids?

We baby boomers have spent the last three decades raising our children in a culture of abandonment. The newfound freedoms of the 1960s and 1970s that we have enjoyed came with a horrible cost. We forgot our kids. The lifestyle changes that came with postmodernism, relativism, and consumerism have mesmerized and drugged us. We get jobs and forget to consider our children in our schedules. We buy good cars, good homes, and good clothes for our children and ourselves and completely forget the job of raising them. We pacify our children with cell phones, iPods, Xboxes, and all the other modern gadgets money can buy. But we neglect the most important thing of all—parenting and fathering.

So who is raising our kids? Who are our children watching? What are they learning? Who are they listening to? Who are their role models? Who are their teachers? Who is constructing their moral foundation? Who are their substitute fathers?

- Television: Statistics have shown that children spend more time watching television than any other activity apart from sleep. The average child sees eight thousand murders on TV before finishing elementary school. By age eighteen, the average child has seen two hundred thousand acts of violence on TV, including forty thousand murders. In a 1995 survey, 62 percent of children aged 10 to 16 said that sex depicted on TV shows and in the movies influences them to have sex when they are young.[1]

- Internet: The Internet has become our children's second teacher. It is accessible twenty-four hours a day to all, including our children. The Internet brings both the good and bad into our homes. The Internet can expose kids to pornography, online harassment, and child predators.

- Peers: The third teacher to our children is their peers. Unfortunately, they are also usually faithful students of television and the Internet.

- Schools: Many parents have abdicated responsibility in raising their children, turning the difficult job over to the teachers and principals in the local schools. "I don't know why that school keeps calling me," one mother once said to another. "I sent him there to learn. They need to take care of his problems and handle him without calling me!" Our endeavor to have our schools single-handedly raise our children has failed. After being interviewed by school administration, a teaching prospect said, "Let me see if I've got this right: You want me to go into that room with all those kids, correct their disruptive behavior, observe them for signs of abuse, monitor their dress habits, censor their T-shirt messages, and instill in them a love for learning. You want me to check their backpacks for weapons, wage war on drugs and sexually transmitted diseases, and raise their sense of self-esteem and personal pride. You want me to teach them patriotism and good citizenship, sportsmanship and fair play, how to register to vote, balance a checkbook, and apply for a job. You want me to check their heads for lice, recognize signs of antisocial behavior, and make sure that they all pass the state exams. You want me to provide them with an equal education regardless of their handicaps, and communicate regularly with their parents by letter, telephone, newsletter, and report card. You want me to do all this with a piece of chalk, a blackboard, a bulletin board, a few books, a big smile, and a starting salary that qualifies me for food stamps. Is that right?"

So how are we baby boomers going to fix the social damage that we have done? First of all, we are going to recognize the problem and start to take responsibility for it. Then we are going to join together parents, sports coaches, teachers, administrators, business people, religious leaders, health-care workers, and government to reconstruct the moral foundation of our children by teaching them about the *virtues* that will help them to live a good life.

Like Aristotle said, "Teachers who educate children deserve more honor than parents who merely gave birth, for bare life is furnished by the one, the other ensures a good life."

Wise Counsel for New Chefs

Counsel is a special gift of advice that can help a young father avoid some of the poor decisions and mistakes of his elders. It is necessary because poor decisions and mistakes can affect others beyond those who just made the poor decisions and mistakes. Sometimes the consequences are extensive and can last for a long time. Most of us can probably think of at least one example of a poor decision that affected a wide circle of individuals, perhaps for generations.

Wise Counsel Often Comes from Elderly Fathers

It is the older generation of fathers who have the opportunity and the responsibility to share their wisdom with the young generation. This is how men can learn to be fathers. It's how we make progress and improvements in living and how a cycle of severe consequences from poor decisions and mistakes can be halted. Elders must tell the young fathers "that something is a bad idea" when they undertake a dangerous or unwise course of action. A man's own father is usually his first elder counselor, and the father may have the responsibility for years without much assistance from anyone else. It is nice if a grandfather is around, because he can provide even a larger frame of wisdom beyond the recent generation.

Wise Counsel May Not Be Well Received

Of course young fathers won't always appreciate a negative directive in regard to what they want to do. Other men in their circle of friends may be encouraging them to make a bad decision. Some men argue that the passage of time invalidates a father's wisdom. The situation is different than in his father's time, a young man might argue, so any decisions won't have the same consequences.

Not All Elders Are Wise All the Time

Some elders also believe that time changes situations. What was a poor decision in their day might be okay now, and the consequences of a chosen course of action were not as bad as they first seemed. Some elders are good at rationalizing their poor decisions and minimizing the consequences of their mistakes. Some still do not like to hear negative comments from others, particularly from a younger father. And most of us can be overly influenced by our emotions, if we are not careful.

Wise Counsel Is More Thoughtful than Good Advice

A person can probably find "good advice" about which lottery tickets to purchase, but "wise counsel" from a mature father would be to "go home and pay off your credit card." What often passes "good advice" is often just foolish opinion.

Wise counsel for fathers comes from individuals who know the difference between

- What is ultimately good and what is just popular
- What is valuable and what is cheap
- A smart investment and quick profit
- What is earned and what is only borrowed
- What is achieved by hard work and what is just lucky
- Being happy and just having fun
- What is beautiful and what just looks attractive
- What is right and what is just legal
- A generous gift and a selfish token
- A sincere apology and a weak excuse
- What is true and what is a matter of opinion,
- Whether to help someone or encourage someone to struggle
- What is love and what is lust
- What is dangerous and what is just risky
- Whether to fight against something or whether to run from it
- A legitimate source of hope and a technique of mass marketing
- A miracle and a magic trick
- What is wise and what is foolish
- A blessing and a temptation
- What lasts forever and what is temporary

The Source of Wise Counsel and Its Superiority

Solomon, the ancient king of Israel who was reputed to be the "wisest man who ever lived," said that the gift of wise counsel—guarding "the course" of your life—is one of the benefits that wise elders give to youth. Solomon said many things about the importance of youth listening to the wise advice of their elders. But he also had some important things to say about the blessings of wisdom to those who have this resource in their lives. He wrote that wisdom "is more profitable than silver and yields better returns than gold."[2] It "is more precious than rubies."[3] "Long life is in her right hand," he wrote. "Her ways are pleasant ways, and all her paths are peace. She is the tree of life to those who embrace her; those who lay hold of her will be blessed."[4]

A Father's Need for Wise Counsel

There certainly can be no doubt that young fathers need the benefits of wise counsel. Many of the basic foundations of social order in the United States are being drastically changed or severely threatened. It may be too late to save some social structures from collapsing after years of poor decisions. But it is never too late to give the gift of wise counsel to those fathers that you can reach.

Burnt Cookies: Shame on Me

Why is the good news about virtue so often rejected by our children? Lots of fathers are fighting the good fight and spreading the good news about virtue to children who need encouragement. But the message is falling on deaf ears, or, even worse, it is thrown right back in their faces. Why?

I contend that it's because, while we think we are sending a message of "salvation," the message is received as one of "damnation." The exact opposite! This is how I think that happens.

People (young and old alike) all carry with them a psychological shadow, sometimes called a "skeleton in the closet." A shadow not reckoned with usually creates either guilt or shame. Guilt says, "I made a mistake." Shame says, " I *am* a mistake."

Shame in Today's Youth Culture

For those fathers working with young people today, there are demographic phenomena to be aware of regarding shame.

- Guilt and shame: Sin is closely connected with shame. Men and women are deeply concerned about what others will think if their misdeeds are discovered. But because shame is associated with exposing actions, a person may think that something is only "wrong" when the action becomes public. Morality therefore becomes strictly external and superficial. The terms *sin* and *sinful* are defined primarily by the public revelation of one's bad actions. For this reason, people are more concerned about losing face than about the bad action and its consequences. Keeping up appearances is more important. They cannot afford to indulge in a true picture of themselves because it would wreck their self-esteem and shame their social circle. So they live in denial, bend the rules, and do anything to keep up appearances.

- The hi-tech era: In the digital age, kids hiding their shadows from people goes into overload. One of the consequences of social media is expanded opportunities for engaging with peers with a false identity. Young people today are on show in far more places, requiring far more choices. The world of social media requires managing an online personality as well as your face-to-face appearance. The demands of social media are relentless. Every minute of the day provides the opportunity (and need) for updating your status. Every status update carries with it the challenge of how you present yourself to the world. And with every "like" or comment, you can track the rise (and fall) of your social standing.

The familiar challenges of adolescent development have combined with changing demographics, postmodern relativism, and technology to create a perfect storm for shame and guilt among teenagers. Here is a world where "what my friends think of me" is not only a constant pressing need, it can be a matter of life and death.

Because moral relativism leaves the culture without a common set of moral standards, today's teenagers believe that, even if they have done something wrong, as long as others believe they haven't, there is little problem because there's no social shame involved. Yet when teenagers believe they have not done anything wrong, if others in the culture think it is wrong, they are left to deal with the resulting shame. This is not healthy for one's soul.

A healthier alternative is to assess our behavior against a common set of moral standards. Then if we believe that we've done the wrong thing, then whether or not others share that belief, we are expected to correct the behavior accordingly. If others say we're guilty of an offense we do not think is wrong, then it is appropriate that we fight the accusation to defend our innocence. This is why we so desperately need to revitalize virtue in our culture and come to agreement on a set of moral standards we can all live with, regardless of faith or theological orientation.

Defending against Exposure of Our Shadows

Unless you feel it is safe to lower your guard and admit your transgressions, you will be defensive of your honor.

Most of us are so embarrassed of our shadows that we:

- Act like hypocrites: The word *hypocrite* derives from the Greek word for acting or pretending. We act, we pretend, and nothing is more self-draining. It takes a lot of spiritual energy to keep that mask on all the time. Every time our public persona contradicts our shadow, we bleed. The spiritual hemorrhaging can be painful.

- Throw stones: We are so embarrassed by our own faults that rather than deal with them, we redirect our attention toward others. Because each of us is imperfect, finding fault in others is the classic pot-calling-the-kettle-black form of hypocrisy.

- Create diversions: We create and engage in diversions to take our mind off of our shadow. These diversions keep us busy, or numb, or both. Gambling, hunting, fishing, golf, exercise, video games, TV, drugs, alcohol, and sex, are a few popular diversions.

- Engage in self-destructive behavior: Self-destructive behavior is often a form of self-punishment in response to facing the ugliness of our shadows. We take to heart our own negative self-talk and negative affirmations from others and punish ourselves in response.

- Harden our hearts: A hardened heart not only poisons the spirit, it literally changes our ability to hear. Messages that are good for us, come across as bad. A message of salvation might come across to us as one of damnation. A message of salvation that is meant to encourage and heal us simply reminds us of our guilt and shame and of how hopeless the struggle to shine the light on our dark shadow is. Rather than being helpful and making us feel good, the message of salvation makes us uncomfortable and even hurts. We take it personally, lash out, become angry and insolent, and vehemently reject the message that could save us.

What can you do to help others soften their hearts and reconcile their shadows to their souls?

- Share your own brokenness. (I have problems just like you)
- Show empathy and offer forgiveness.
- Share the anonymous brokenness of a group. (We have problems just like you)
- Be quiet and let someone tell you his or her story.
- Tell a heartrending story or parable that challenges perceptions about redemption.
- Let this person know that you can help reconcile the shadow and, if necessary, transform his or her existence to something better.

- Be physically present. You don't have to say or do anything, just be there.
- Demonstrate unconditional love.

As fathers engage in bringing the good news of encouragement, virtue, and salvation to their children, we do better to start with actions designed to soften their hearts and create opportunities for redemption, rather than trying to prematurely shove the good fruits of virtue down their throats.

2

BEEF

When I think about cooking beef, the first thing that comes to mind is a big, juicy T-bone steak cooked on the barbecue, with a baked potato and some butter-fried mushrooms on the side. Steak is probably my favorite way to eat beef, but there are plenty of other cuts that I love to cook and eat. Prime rib, meat loaf, brisket, jerky, hamburgers—there are so many fantastic options.

The first thing to know is what makes a piece of beef. There's actually a lot going on! But to know how to cook beef, you need to know three main things:

- *Beef is a muscle, so it's full of protein. The protein molecules go through many changes when you cook your piece of beef. The first thing that happens is that they bunch together into fibers. Then, as you cook the beef, the fibers lose moisture and shrink, making your meat tougher.*

- *Every piece of beef has some fat in it, some more than others. When you cook your piece of beef, the fat creates a protective layer around your protein fibers, which helps prevent the meat from drying out. It also adds a lot of flavor. I always go for the well-marbled cut.*

- *Meat is actually mostly made up of water. A piece of beef is 60 to 75 percent water! When you cook a piece of beef, some of that water is lost. But the less water you lose, the juicier the beef you end up with. So it's important not to overcook your beef.*

Prime Rib

Ingredients:

One prime rib roast

Traeger Prime Rib Rub or Montreal steak seasoning

Preparation:

Rub prime rib liberally with Traeger Prime Rib Rub or Montreal steak seasoning. Put it on heavy. Place prime rib in a plastic bag and refrigerate overnight.

Method:

Remove from refrigerator 1 hour before serving.

Fire your grill and set to high. Let the grill preheat for 15 minutes.

Place prime rib on the grill fat side up and cook on high for 30 minutes.

After 30 minutes, turn grill down to medium speed (225°–250°)[1] and cook for 3 hours.

Monitor internal temperature at thickest part of prime rib with a meat probe thermometer.

To figure out the total cooking time, allow about 13 to 15 minutes per pound for rare and 15 to 17 minutes per pound for medium rare. The actual cooking time will depend on the shape of the roast, the outside temperature, and your particular grill.

Cook the prime rib until thermometer registers 115° to 120° for rare, or 125° to 130° for medium.

Remove from grill, slice, and serve. Don't forget the horseradish!

I recommend mesquite wood pellets for prime ribs.

[1] All temperatures are Fahrenheit.

Steak

Ingredients:

Rib-eye steaks

Olive oil—2 tablespoons (as needed)

Traeger Prime Rib Rub or Montreal steak seasoning

Bourbon—1 tablespoon (more or less as needed)

Preparation:

Preheat grill to 375°.

Drizzle oil on both sides of meat and rub Prime Rib Rub or Montreal steak seasoning over all.

Drizzle bourbon over the steaks and let rest for a few minutes.

Method:

Place the steaks on the grill and cook until internal temperature reaches 135° (medium rare).

Remove meat from grill and let rest for a few minutes before carving.

I recommend mesquite wood pellets for steaks.

Meat Loaf

Ingredients:

1 1/2 pounds ground beef

1 1/2 pounds ground pork

2 cups dry bread crumbs

1/2 cup finely chopped sweet onion

1/2 cup finely chopped green pepper

1 egg, beaten

1 teaspoon Worcestershire sauce

1 teaspoon minced garlic

1 teaspoon Traeger Prime Rib Rub or Montreal steak seasoning

1 teaspoon ground black pepper

1/2 cup ketchup

Preparation:

Preheat the grill at 300° and scrape the grates clean. Spray grates with nonstick cooking spray.

In a bowl, mix together all the ingredients.

Form the meat into a loaf about 2 inches thick.

Method:

Place the meat loaf directly on the grill. Cook until the loaf reaches an internal temperature of at least 160°, about 1.5 hours. Toward the end of the cook time, spread barbecue sauce or ketchup on the top of the loaf.

Remove from the grill, slice and serve.

Jerky

Ingredients:

4 tablespoons ground black pepper

1 cup soy sauce

1 tablespoon apple cider vinegar

1 dash hot pepper sauce

1 dash Worcestershire sauce

2 pounds sirloin, cut into 1/2 inch thick slices

Preparation:

In a large bowl, combine the ground black pepper, soy sauce, vinegar, hot pepper sauce, and Worcestershire sauce. Mix well and add the meat slices. Cover and refrigerate overnight.

Set your grill to smoke, and lightly oil the grates.

Method:

Lay meat strips out on grill so that they do not overlap. Smoke over low heat (170°–190°). Jerky will be done when the edges appear dry with just a slight hint of moisture in the center of the slices, about 6 to 8 hours.

Beef Brisket

Ingredients:

1 beef brisket (5 to 6 pounds), with a layer of fat at least 1/4 inch thick on one side

Traeger Prime Rib Rub or Montreal steak seasoning

One bottle spicy honey barbecue sauce

One table spoon red pepper flakes

1 cup apple cider vinegar

Preparation:

Rinse the brisket under cold running water and blot it dry with paper towels.

Rub the Traeger Prime Rib Rub or Montreal steak seasoning liberally on the brisket on all sides. Wrap the brisket in a plastic bag and let it cure in the refrigerator overnight.

Method:

Preheat your grill to 325°.

Place the brisket, fat side up, directly on the grill. Cook at 325° for 1 hour.

After 1 hour, turn the grill down to 225°. Cook at 225° for 4 hours.

After 4 hours, mix the sauce by combining the spicy honey barbecue sauce, apple cider vinegar, and red pepper flakes.

Remove the brisket from the grill and place in a 2-inch-deep disposable aluminum pan. Pour the mixed sauce over the top of the brisket. Cover and seal the brisket in the aluminum pan with tin foil and return it to the grill.

Continue cooking 225° for two more hours or until the brisket is tender enough to shred with your fingers. The cooking time will depend on the size of the brisket and the outside temperature.

Remove the brisket pan from the grill and let rest for 15 minutes. Transfer the brisket to a cutting board and thinly slice it across the grain, using a sharp knife, an electric knife, or a cleaver. Transfer the sliced meat to a platter, pour any remaining sauce on top, and serve at once.

I recommend mesquite wood pellets for beef brisket.

3

FOR BROTHERS

Sometimes it's easy to take your brother for granted, or to be hard on him. Yet for many people who have a brother, it can be a good thing to take stock of his good qualities, to recognize all the great things he does for you and others, and to give him a morale boost that shows you care about him and are glad he's your brother. When you think about the good things your brother does, you set aside the things you find annoying, bothersome, and unfair. Try to put aside any sense of competition or desire to avoid him and simply list what he does really well.

With these qualities in mind, to be a manly brother you will:

- Arrange to spend time with siblings. Whether you live together or apart, making a specific time together and share stories, jokes, and tales is a great way to reconnect without the usual hubbub of sibling life around you. If you're still at home, arrange a walk to the park together or something similar that you'll both enjoy. If you live apart, make a time to meet in a local cafe or one another's homes to catch up over coffee or a meal.

- Be there for your siblings during tough times. Life doesn't always go according to plan, and there will be times when they need you. Be there for them and be supportive when they experience relationship, job, health, or other problems. In turn, they are more likely to be there for you.

- Back down from trivial and pointless arguments. There are bound to be arguments occasionally between siblings, and they can strike at any age. Instead of continuing to engage in a fighting mood, know which battles are worth pursuing and which are best left alone. When you argue, try to compromise and see your sibling's side of things. You might just shock your brother or sister into seeing your point of view as well!

- Treat your siblings with the kindness and respect you expect from them. Show by example the kind of relationship you'd like and refuse to fall into argumentative or bossy patterns of relating to each other.

- Stand up for your siblings and their special life events. Sometimes a sibling might need your support in a public way. Demonstrate that your brother or sister is someone you trust and believe in.

- Don't be a nag, a telltale, or a nuisance. Like everyone else, your siblings might become riled if they think they're being told on, prattled at, or bothered constantly. Aim to give your siblings the space they need to get on with their lives, and expect them to do the same for you. While it's nice to spend time together, don't crowd a brother or sister as if you had to be best friends. And when you feel a need to tell a sibling what to do all the time, imagine how that kind of treatment would annoy you.

- Give your siblings a big hug. When you hug them, tell them that you love them and are proud of them. You don't need an excuse to do this; whenever it happens is a good time. Try not to hold back praise for your siblings. When you notice something great they have done, let them know it.

Helping Others Cook

If we are going to live a virtuous life, we must turn away from vice every time it tries to peck at our soul. We must also break the chains that vice has on our hearts and extinguish the fires of temptation that are sparked in our souls. To do this, quite often we must turn our backs on the ways of the world and the social acceptance of supposed friends. This is a hard thing for most of us to do because at heart, we are all brothers.

"Turn away from vice!" It's a simple phrase that is easy to say and hard to do. The best that we can hope to accomplish will be difficult and gradual. We each must fight our own personal battle against it. Sometimes we need help from friends and family, but more often than not, we fight the most difficult battles in the private recesses of our own hearts and souls. There the battles rage with volleys of suffering, pain, self-denial, victories, losses, and personal heroism.

To effectively win our soul's battle with vice, we often rely on these strategies:

- We separate ourselves from friends or associates who practice vice. Birds of a feather flock together. Find new friends or associates who are virtuous.

- We avoid or run from situations in which we are tempted to sin. This includes avoiding events or places where vice lives. Don't go. Leave now.

- We become cognizant of which vices have their hooks in us. We learn to discipline ourselves, and to repress and cut off these attachments. We know our weaknesses.

- We extinguish the fires of temptation when they are a tiny spark, before they grow into an inferno. We exhibit self-control.

- We discipline our senses by practicing small acts of self-deprivation. We become the master of our emotions, rather than a slave to them.

- We die to ourselves by serving others.

To turn away from vice, the price is high: we must position ourselves courageously against human nature, against the world, and against the approval of our modern society. It's no easy thing to conquer our passions, emotions, weaknesses, and temptations. However, every time we have a victory over vice, it strengthens our soul. When our soul becomes strong, the temptations that do come touch only the soul's surface. They do not penetrate and gain a foothold. When they are gone, we experience the joy of victory, achieved by the strengthening of our own will and the conquering of temptation. Only then do we stand ready to serve our fellow man as strong and generous souls.

Cooking Tips from the World's Best Chefs

All great men have a beginner's mind. They come to terms with humility and shortcomings. With a beginner's mind, a man responds to each moment as it arises, without prejudice, expectations, or baggage, approaching life's situations with openness and innocence.

Here are three powerful phrases to help you approach life with a beginner's mind:

- "I don't know. What do you think?" Be done thinking that you are all things to all people. You don't have to have the answer. Many things in life are simply a mystery, and there is no right answer. It's good enough to just sit with the question.

- "I am happy with what I have; it's good enough." It always seems that what we have is never good enough. There is always more to achieve, gain, and earn. There is a great peace that comes with being grateful for what we have and not longing for what we don't have, and saying, without regrets, longing, or sense of being incomplete, "I'm good and that's enough."

- "I could be wrong." We all want to be right in everything that we say and do. But we don't have to be right all the time. Sometimes what we think is right is wrong. We don't have to know everything.

Forgive Offenses

Let go of any anger, resentment, or emotional injuries that you may be harboring. Soften that hardened heart and forgive those who have wronged you. The freedom you will experience from forgiving is cleansing and joyous. It is also important to forgive yourself for your own wrongdoings. You are not perfect. People will still love you in spite of your imperfections.

Five Spiritual Truths

- Life is hard. There will be times of suffering, pain, loss, and hurt. Accept these difficulties as times of growth. You will survive. That which doesn't kill you makes you stronger.
- You are not in control. You may have thought that you were in control, but, in fact, you were never in control.
- Your body is going to die. What's going to happen to your soul when it does?
- You are not all that important. The world doesn't revolve around you. People will forget about you real fast when you are gone.
- Your life is not about you. There is a great story unfolding before you. You are a small player in that story, but the story is big, cosmic, and sacred. Your job is to live the role in that story that God predestined for you.

Characteristics of Wise Brothers

- Wise brothers are quiet, secure, and patient, with little to prove and much to teach.
- Wise brothers can see beyond youth's transitory illusions of possessions, money, and power.
- Wise bothers allow life to flow in the patterns it chooses. "Float like a leaf down the river of life."

- Wise brothers joyfully accept a limited world.
- Wise brothers are able to cry from the heart and laugh from the belly.
- Wise brothers enjoy the moment without worrying about long-range consequences.
- Wise brothers know that the best classroom in the world is at the feet of an elderly person.
- Wise brothers know that the easiest way for you to grow as a person is to surround yourself with people who are smarter that you.

Appetizers

When it comes to living as a virtuous man, we often find ourselves being able to "talk the talk," but we have a hard time "walking the walk." We wholeheartedly commit ourselves to loving and serving our fellow man but either deliberately or through ignorance let opportunities for loving others pass. It's almost like we sleepwalk past these opportunities. Wake up! Come alive by doing small acts of love for others. The opportunities are in front of us dozens of times each day, like choosing something small from the menu as an appetizer.

We need to open our eyes and become attentive to the needs and suffering of people who present themselves in our daily lives. If we really and truly love others as ourselves, should we sit around and wait for them to ask us to do something for them? Or, by being aware of other's needs and seeing something that needs doing, shouldn't we just do it?

There is an old story that illustrates this very well. A family suffered the tragic loss of a child. It was the family's custom to leave their shoes outside the back door. A man who knew this family heard of their loss. When he came to the family's house to offer his condolences, he saw the shoes outside the door. It occurred to him that they might want to wear those shoes to the funeral. The shoes were worn and dirty, so he took them home, cleaned and shined them, and returned them before they'd been missed.

The opportunity to do a small act of love presented itself to him and he took action.

"I knew if I had asked if there was anything I could do, they would have said no. Their shoes needed cleaning so I did it," he said matter-of-factly. To him it was no big deal, but to the family, his "small act of love" touched their hearts and eased their pain. Pain is a lot easier to handle when you know people love you.

Stop and think back over your day: Was there something you needed to do but didn't because you would have been socially embarrassed to act? Was there a person who would have loved a five-minute talk but you were too busy with mundane tasks that could have waited? Did you miss an opportunity to help an elderly person? How many people did you walk by who looked dejected and needed an encouraging word? Was there something that you could have done for your parents that would have made them smile? Could you have taken five minutes of your time to help another student struggling with a math problem?

Every day we are given opportunities to change the world with "small acts of love." But we may fail to see those opportunities because we're too busy, stressed, or caught up in our own lives. Open your eyes to the needs of others, have the courage to do what needs to be done, and don't fool yourself by thinking that the "small acts of love" are too insignificant to make a difference.

Remember the story of the little boy who was seen throwing starfish that had washed up on the beach back into the ocean? "Why do you bother?" a man asked him. "There are hundreds of them. You couldn't possibly save them all." "No," the little boy answered as he threw the starfish back into the sea, "but I can save this one, and it makes a difference to him."

What you do (or don't do) each day does make a difference in the lives of others.

A Great Cookbook

From the beginning of time, man has been trying to make sense of himself and his world. He has been seeking understanding. But as time marches on, man isn't finding the understanding he seeks; he isn't happier, and he hasn't been able to conquer his own nature. What's wrong? With all the great minds that have gone before us, with all the lessons of history left for us to examine, it's hard to imagine why we aren't further along than we are. In our search for meaning, why are we asking the same questions the ancient Greeks were asking 2,600 years ago? Don't we have enough information available by now to find the answers?

Technology inundates us daily with more information than we can possibly process. We are suffering from information overload. There are so many unwanted messages bombarding us, that, quite often, the ones we need get lost in the noise. The average person can now communicate faster, with more people—without thinking—than ever before.

So what are we doing with all this information? Is it really doing us any good? Are we living happier lives? Are we experiencing fewer problems? Are our decisions better? Are we any wiser? History tells us that we haven't learned much in spite of all we know. The situation changes, but the problems remain the same.

The answer is that we need wisdom more than we need information or knowledge. Information is data that's been collected and organized. It is a reference tool that we turn to when trying to create something else. A glut of information can be counterproductive. While it adds to our knowledge, it can be a block to our wisdom. We can be so busy trying to process more and more information that we don't have the time for the quiet contemplation that is essential for the development of wisdom. Without contemplation, we lose our perspective; we don't know where we are going—we just go!

Knowledge is information that we have digested and understand. It can deceive us into thinking we are wise, but knowledge alone is not wisdom. For example, have you ever known someone who is incredibly smart? Maybe they get straight A's in school, or maybe they have several degrees, and yet their life is a complete mess. What's wrong? These people aren't dumb. They don't seem to lack the necessary information to be a success in life. Yet life for them is one struggle after another. Sadly, they lack wisdom. For the successful conduct of life, mere knowledge is not enough.

Neither information nor knowledge is wisdom. There is a big difference. Wisdom is knowledge that has been applied in a way that takes into account all its pertinent relationships and is consistent with virtue. To have wisdom is to have a long-term perspective, to see the big picture, and to look beyond the immediate situation. Wisdom is practicing what you have learned rather than constantly seeking to learn new things (that you probably will never put into practice). Remember the phrase "All I needed to learn, I learned in kindergarten"? A man possesses wisdom and eloquence only in proportion to the virtue that he actually practices.

You can talk all day long about being wise and virtuous, but if you don't put that virtue into action, your wisdom is wasted. Ask yourself, what did I learn today about virtue? How can I transfer this lesson to my own life? How can I apply it? You then begin to live intelligently, with understanding, meaning, and wisdom.

4

POULTRY

Poultry is one of the most versatile meats you can put on the grill. Easy to cook and capable of taking on almost any flavor, it also has the added attraction of being low-fat and able to take most any seasoning.

When it comes to grilling, most people grill either breasts, parts, or the whole bird.

When grilling chicken breasts, it is important to work with an evenly thick piece of meat. Pound your skinless, boneless chicken breast to a uniform thickness so that it will cook through the middle without drying on the ends. Chicken breasts are virtually fat free and a great healthy food, but you need to prevent drying. To do this it is best to use a marinade on your chicken breasts. Grill uniformly thin and marinated skinless, boneless chicken breasts on high (325°–350°).[2]

Grill other chicken pieces, like legs and thighs, slower. As the fats in these heat up and drain out, you will get flare-ups. To prevent this, lower the temperature and let the chicken grill slowly.

When you want to cook a whole chicken or turkey, simply place it on the grill and cook it at a medium heat of 300°–325°.

When you add sauces, particularly sweet sauces, do so toward the end of the cooking time and lower the temperature to 265° or less so that the sugars don't burn.

2[*] All temperatures are Fahrenheit.

BBQ Chicken

Ingredients:

Traeger Chicken Rub or Morton's Sugar Cure (do not use the spice pack shipped in the bag)

1 whole chicken, 4 to 5 pounds, neck, giblets, and excess fat removed

Preparation:

Wash the chicken in cold water and pat dry with a paper towel.

Cut the chicken into eight pieces: two breast pieces, two thigh pieces, two drumsticks, and two wings. Remove and discard the wing tips.

Pour the rub or spices into a bowl. Wet your hands, place some spice on your fingers, and *lightly* rub down the chicken pieces. Be sure to lightly cover the pieces. A little goes a long way.

Set the grill at 325°.

Method:

Grill the chicken pieces, skin side up, with the lid closed, until the juices run clear and the meat is no longer pink at the bone. The drumsticks and thighs will take 40 to 50 minutes and the breasts and wings will take 30 to 40 minutes. If you want barbecue sauce on the chicken, put it on during the last 10 to 15 minutes of grilling time, turning the pieces once or twice during this period. Remove from the grill and serve warm.

Smoked Teriyaki Turkey

Ingredients:

1/8 cup Traeger Chicken Rub or Morton's Sugar Cure

1 1/4 cups packed dark brown sugar

1 (12- to 15-pound) turkey, thawed if frozen

1 medium-sized ginger root, sliced into 1/8-inch slices

16 oz. Mr. Yoshida's Original Teriyaki Sauce

Preparation:

Start this recipe the night before by brining the turkey. Then smoke the bird the next day.

Remove giblets and neck from the turkey cavity and discard.

Remove any wire or plastic holding the legs together.

Rinse the turkey inside and out with cold water.

Rub the turkey down with the Traeger Chicken Rub or Morton's Sugar Cure.

Place the turkey in a large plastic bag. Pour in brown sugar, ginger root, and teriyaki sauce. Close the top of the bag and swish the brine over the turkey. Tie off the bag and refrigerate overnight.

The next day, remove the turkey from the brine bag, rinse with cold water, and pat dry with paper towels.

Method:

Fire the grill and set on 225°.

Tuck the wing tips back and underneath the drumettes to form two triangles.

Place the turkey, breast-side up, on the grill. Cover and cook at 225°.

Cook until the internal temperature reads 165° on a meat thermometer inserted into the thickest part of the breast and thigh (make sure it's not touching the bone), about 2 to 3 hours, depending on the outside temperature. When the turkey is done, remove it from the grill, transfer it to a cutting board or baking sheet, and immediately baste with melted butter. Tent the turkey with foil and let it rest for at least 10 minutes.

Boneless Chicken Thighs

Ingredients:

1/3 cup soy sauce

1/4 Mr. Yoshida's Original Teriyaki Sauce

3 tablespoons minced garlic

1 tablespoon black pepper

8 boneless chicken thighs

Preparation:

Whisk the spice and sauce ingredients and pour the marinade into a large plastic zipper bag.

Place the chicken thighs into the bag containing marinade, squeeze all the air out of the bag, and seal. Shake a few times to coat chicken.

Refrigerate for 1 hour, turning bag once or twice.

Preheat the grill to 325°.

Method:

Remove the chicken from the bag; discard the marinade.

Place chicken thighs onto the grill. Cook for 30 minutes until done; an instant-read thermometer inserted into a chicken thigh should read 165°. Let stand for 5 or 10 minutes and then serve.

I recommend hickory or alder wood pellets for this recipe.

Chicken Quesadillas

Ingredients:

8 flour tortillas

1 pound mozzarella cheddar blend cheese, shredded

1/2 package Old El Paso Fajita Seasoning Mix

2 or 3 boneless skinless chicken breasts

Cilantro salsa, sour cream, and guacamole to taste

Preparation:

Rub down the chicken breasts with the Old El Paso Fajita Seasoning Mix.

Fire grill and set at 350°.

Method:

Place chicken breasts on the grill and cook about 15 to 20 minutes.

After chicken is cooked, remove from grill and let cool.

Slice chicken breasts into small half-inch chunks.

Place a tortilla directly on the grill.

Layer ingredients in the following order on half of the tortilla: cheese and then chicken.

When the cheese starts to melt, it is time to fold the tortilla. Fold the empty half of the tortilla over top of the side with the cheese and chicken.

Be careful to keep everything together while flipping. Don't burn yourself. Use tongs or a spatula.

Turn over once. Shell should be toasty and a golden color. Remove from the grill.

Let stand for a few moments and then cut into quarters, serve with your choice of sour cream, guacamole, or salsa for dipping.

5

FOR TEAMMATES AND COWORKERS

A good teammate or coworker understands that no matter what position you play, whether you are the best player on the team or on the field, you are nothing without your teammates. The key to being a good teammate or coworker is being willing to give up anything for your team, sacrificing whatever it takes.

Being a good teammate is very important. Anyone can throw on a jersey and call herself part of the team, but there is so much more to it than that. When you put on your jersey, you are not only becoming part of a team but part of a family. Whether you get along or not, all your problems should be pushed aside for the sake of your team. Teammates are supposed to be responsible for one another and look out for each other on and off the field. A good teammate should be willing to sacrifice anything for the sake of the team. The best teammates are ones who pull for each other, even while competing for a position. You should continue to root your teammate on because you are both vital to the team's success. There is no room for negativity on a team. A good teammate should never put another player down; teammates should always pick each other up, especially on their lowest days. Teammates stick together, even on their worst days. No matter what a player may go through, just think how much more difficult it would be alone.

Being committed to a team is the same as being committed to a job. Your coworkers rely on you to be there, and they expect you to work hard to become your best. Becoming your best for the sake of the whole is a great teammate quality and also a valuable lifelong trait. This, along with the other teammate traits mentioned, builds character and shapes us for a future of happiness and success.

Winners versus Losers

- Winners say, "We can do it." Losers say, "We can try it."
- Winners look for continued improvement. Losers are overly proud of the way things are now.
- Winners look for opportunities. Losers sit and wait for the next thing to go wrong.
- Winners *play* a good game. Losers *talk* a good game.
- Winners judge themselves. Losers hope others will judge them favorably.
- Winners know that they must confront problems head on. Losers choose not to act, hoping the problem will go away.
- Winners treat others with respect, as they would like to be treated. Losers look out for themselves and don't care about others.
- Winners say, "I'm responsible for that." Losers say "It's not my fault."
- Winners can laugh at themselves. Losers are offended by humor directed at them.
- A winner shares credit. A loser wants all the credit.
- A winner says, "I'll take the blame." A loser looks for someone else to blame.
- The winner is a tireless worker. The loser is a tired worker.
- When things get tough, the winner is overwhelming. When things get tough, the loser is overwhelmed.
- The winner goes for "the win." The loser goes for "the tie."

- The winner rises above adversity. The loser runs from adversity.
- Winners say, "We can fix that." Losers say, "I told you that wouldn't work."
- Winners are success-oriented, ready to adapt their procedures in an attempt to win. Losers can't see past the procedure and complain about any change.
- Winners provide direction. Losers give orders.
- Winners earn respect. Losers demand respect.
- Winners teach. Losers pontificate.
- Winners manage the stress in their home lives. Losers are managed by the stress in their home lives.
- Winners make the rules work for them. Losers always go strictly by the rules.
- Winners work hard all the time. Losers spend time avoiding hard work.
- Winners attempt to be objective and look at the facts. Losers are emotional and can be swayed and influenced by others.
- Winners are here to serve. Losers want to be served.
- Winners enjoy their time at work. Losers put in their time and go home.
- A winner will fight to keep his or her position. A loser doesn't care and would rather complain than work to regain the position.

Artificial Ingredients

A couple of outdated words in the English language that I think we should bring back and use more are *fain* (to want, to desire) and *feign* (to pretend or act). I am talking here about feigned ingredients.

Some of my favorite writings are those of Blaise Pascal (1623–1662), a French mathematician, physicist, inventor, and philosopher. On man's hatred of the truth regarding his own character, Pascal wrote:

> Man would fain be great and sees that he is little; would fain be happy and sees that he is miserable; would fain be perfect and sees that he is full of imperfections; would fain be the object of love and esteem of men, and sees that his faults merit only their aversion and contempt. The embarrassment wherein he finds himself produces in him the most unjust and criminal passions imaginable, for he conceives a mortal hatred against the truth which blames him and convinces him of his faults.

We are so embarrassed by the truth of our own shortcomings that it produces in us the most unjust and criminal passions imaginable. These unjust and criminal passions manifest themselves as pride, greed, vanity, lust, apathy, envy, wrath, anger, rage, and violence. We lash out with lying tongues, hurt innocent people, devise wicked plots, run to trouble, become deceitful witnesses, and sow discord wherever we go.

Even worse, we look in the mirror and deny the truth about ourselves. We pretend, we feign rather than act with sincerity.

Real sincerity means forgiving ourselves and humbling ourselves in the face of our human errors. It means looking our faults in the eye and seeing all their horror, dirt, meanness, and malice. Then, after forgiving ourselves, we commit to change, reformation, and living more virtuous lives.

If we avoided the artificial ingredients, we would be free to live life with the sincerity that brings peace to our souls.

Lead Chefs and the Kitchen Crew

You have probably heard the old cliché that teams emulate life. But it is true, and I think gets to the heart of why we value the teamwork so highly. Just like life, teams are about death and resurrection. It's about the teammates' transformation from a lower physical, temporal, selfish, ego-driven self to a higher spiritual, self-sacrificing team self. To have a great team, individual players must die to themselves and sacrifice their wills, their bodies, and their lives for the team. The well-known poem by James Patrick Kinney, written in the 1960s during the civil rights movement, brings this point home.

The Cold Within

Six humans trapped by happenstance
In bleak and bitter cold.
Each one possessed a stick of wood
Or so the story's told.

Their dying fire in need of logs
The first man held his back
For of the faces round the fire
He noticed one was black.

The next man looking 'cross the way
Saw one not of his church,
And couldn't bring himself to give
The fire his stick of birch.

The third one sat in tattered clothes.
He gave his coat a hitch.
Why should his log be put to use
To warm the idle rich?

The rich man just sat back and thought
Of the wealth he had in store
And how to keep what he had earned
From the lazy, shiftless poor.

The black man's face spoke revenge
As the fire passed from his sight.
For all he saw in his stick of wood
Was a chance to spite the white.

The last man of this forlorn group
Did naught except for gain,
Giving only to those who gave
Was how he played the game.

Their logs held tight in death's still hands
Was proof of human sin.
They didn't die from the cold without,
They died from the cold within.

On every team, just like in life, the self must be denied because our carnal mind is driven by pride and an underlying belief and desire that we must get things for ourselves. This is the way of the world, the way of vanity, self-centeredness, coveting, greed, envy, and defeat. To achieve victory, players and teammates must serve as living sacrifices by loving and serving each other. We must put to death our carnal, selfish minds and replace "me" with a unified "we" mentality based on love and servitude.

This is not the way of the world. It's hard to die to one's self and deny that carnal ego. It's a lot easier to go along with the way of the world. That is why I believe the rosters of teams that are categorically labeled as "losers" are probably full of of players who are more concerned about "me" than "we."

Where does your team stand?

Gentle Chefs

Have you ever heard the Bible verse, "A bruised reed He will not break"?[5] Can you picture the bruised reed? It is fragile and easily shaken by the wind. Bent over and discolored, it was beaten and broken by some force. Maybe someone charged through a cattail marsh and thrashed a stick, bashing the cattails to the side to clear the way, leaving a clearly marked trail of destruction in their wake. Sometimes it seems our world is full of people like that.

The bruised reed represents those around us who are hurting, spiritually weak, or of little faith. They need to be treated with gentleness until their true need is exposed and they open up to ask for help. Maybe they are battling a physical illness or experiencing difficulties in their relationships. They may be discouraged, grieving, angry, embarrassed, worried, longing, hoping, waiting, empty, battered, and bruised. Shouldn't we approach each other with the utmost gentleness until we learn more about what's at the heart of a person's spirit?

People are at ease around a truly gentle person. If you would like to help people who are hurting and in need, you first need to practice gentleness. Bruised reeds will sense your gentleness and open the door to their spirit. At first that door may be open only a small crack, but with time and trust, they will usually open fully. In fact, in today's harsh society, bruised reeds usually flock to people known for their gentleness.

So how do we develop gentleness in our lives? It is not a natural characteristic. It is a gift from the Spirit. It must be sought. Then gentleness must be applied in our lives. How will gentleness manifest itself in our lives?

- We actively seek to make others feel at ease, being sensitive to their opinions and ideas.
- We show respect for the personal dignity of others. When we feel compelled to change a wrong opinion, we do so with gentle persuasion and kindness rather than domination and intimidation.
- We avoid blunt speech and an abrupt manner, being sensitive to how others react to our words. When it is necessary to provide correction, we build it on a foundation of encouragement.
- We won't be threatened by opposition, but gently wait for the opposition to be dissolved over time.
- We do not belittle, degrade, or gossip about a brother or sister who has stumbled and succumbed to vice. But we gently encourage them and patiently pray for their repentance.
- We are particularly gentle with our mates, children, families, and friends—the ones we say we love.
- We are gentle in the way we care for ourselves and set expectations for ourselves.

It serves us well to remember that, in one way or another, we are all bruised reeds. That is why, if for no other reason, we should be gentle people and gentlemen, with good manners and respect for one another. Virtuous teammates and coworkers should shine forth as lights in the world by emulating gentleness in word and deed.

Kitchen Enthusiasm: Fake It 'Til You Make It

A lack of enthusiasm is like a virus. Take a look at any team, business, class, school, parish, organization, or even a home. When times are tough, many people share their pessimism, fears, and general lack of enthusiasm with their teammates, fellow coaches, classmates, teachers, parishioners, suppliers, customers, and family members. This lack of enthusiasm quickly spreads like a virus, creating in its wake one of the most damaging problems a team, school, business, parish, or family can face—a lack of faith!

"Fake it 'til you make it" is a common catchphrase that can inspire us to imitate enthusiasm. As it is then observed by others, it produces real enthusiasm in the people around us. The phrase can also be a useful tool to help us avoid a self-fulfilling prophecy related to fears about lacking enthusiasm.

Great leaders are often called on to create enthusiasm where there is none. They may need to bring newfound enthusiasm to the mundane tasks of daily life, particularly when things are boring, depressing, or haven't been going well. Being that spark of enthusiasm who sets afire the spirits of your team, class, organization, or family can be difficult.

Here are two examples of how a leader can be a spark of enthusiasm.

On a team: There will be days when things are not going well and you find your team down in the dumps. On the field you see fear or apathy in the eyes of your players and assistant coaches. You may feel the same way, but your obligation as a leader is to rekindle the fire of enthusiasm. Fake it or blow smoke until the fire ignites. It's been said that you have to be a champion before you can win a championship. Spark your team into displaying the enthusiasm of a champion rather than the fear of a loser. Fake it till you make it.

At work: It's no secret that business has been tough since the recession of 2008–2009. But the businesses that are making it are the ones that have kept their enthusiasm. Customers feel confident buying products from upbeat enthusiastic businesses. Even when times are bad, fake it till you make it. Positive enthusiasm generates a buzz. Customers sense the positive activity and go out of their way to spread the good news and fire up new customers for you.

Initially, creating enthusiasm from nothing can feel forced, but if you continue throwing off those sparks, a fire will start in the people around you and in your own heart. Suddenly, before you realize it, your fake enthusiasm has become real. You have created a positive feedback loop that is now generating its own energy.

George C. Marshall said, "It is not enough to fight. It is the spirit which we bring to the fight that decides the issue. It's morale that wins the victory."[6]

That spirit, that it is morale that wins, is created by enthusiasm, which can be sparked with as little as a smile and a few upbeat words to your fellow teammate. Being enthusiastic isn't that difficult, and it can result in a chain reaction of good in the world. So, if you have to, fake it till you make it.

6

PORK

Pork truly is the "other white meat," as the National Pork Board's advertising campaign used to say. Many cuts of fresh pork are leaner today than they were two decades ago—on average, about 16 percent lower in total fat and 27 percent lower in saturated fat. Seven cuts of pork meet USDA's guidelines for "lean" or "extra lean." An easy way to remember lean cuts is to look for the word "loin" on the label, such as loin chop or pork tenderloin.

Barbecuing is the preferred method of cooking pork. The pork takes on the smoky flavor of the wood fire, which enhances the taste appeal. Pork is frequently basted with a tangy tomato- or vinegar-based sauce.

A serving size of pork is three ounces, which is roughly equal in size to a deck of cards. If you are working with lean ribs, like back ribs, serving size will be about 3 to 4 ribs, including the bone. Thicker and heavier cuts like spareribs will be closer to 1 to 2 ribs per serving.

Cook pork to 160°.[3] Reheat precooked ham to 140° or enjoy it cold.

Spareribs

Ingredients:

2 slabs pork spareribs, about 6 pounds total

2 tablespoons vegetable oil

---

[3] All temperatures are Fahrenheit.

Traeger Chicken Rub or Traeger Pork & Poultry Seasoning

Barbecue sauce sweet and spicy

Apple cider vinegar

Preparation:

Remove the membrane on the back (bone side) of the ribs.

Rub ribs with Traeger Chicken Rub or Traeger Pork & Poultry Seasoning.

Sprinkle on a little vegetable oil and smear around lightly.

Turn on the grill at set at 250°.

Method:

Place ribs, not overlapping on the grill. Cook ribs for 1 1/2 to 2 hours, until ribs are very tender.

Mix the barbecue sauce with about ¼ cup of apple cider vinegar.

In final 15–20 minutes of grilling, remove the ribs from the grill, baste them with barbecue/vinegar sauce, and wrap in aluminum foil. Return to the grill for the remaining time.

Cut and serve ribs.

Pork Shoulder

Ingredients:

3 pounds bone-in pork shoulder roast

Morton's Sugar Cure

Barbecue sauce sweet and spicy

Apple cider vinegar

Preparation:

Rub the pork shoulder with Morton's Sugar Cure.

Turn on the grill at set at 250°.

Method:

Place the pork shoulder on the grill to cook.

Slow cook for 4 hours.

At four hours, remove the shoulder from the grill and place in a small disposable aluminum pan.

Mix the sweet and spicy barbecue sauce with the apple cider vinegar.

Baste the pork shoulder with the barbecue/vinegar sauce liberally.

Seal the top of the pan with aluminum foil and return to the grill.

Cook 1–2 more hours (depending on the outside temperature) until the meat is fall-off-the-bone tender.

Slice and serve, or pull apart into small pieces for pulled pork sandwiches.

Bone-In Ham

Ingredients:

1 bone-in country ham (cured, smoked, and aged, required to be cooked before eating)

or

1 picnic ham (from the front leg instead of the back; it is less tender and has more fat)

Morton's Sugar Cure

Brown sugar

Pineapple slices

Preparation:

Rub down the ham with the Morton's Sugar Cure.

With wooden toothpicks, pin the pineapple slices on the top and sides of the ham.

Sprinkle brown sugar over the pineapple slices.

Fire the grill and set at 250°.

Method:

Place the ham on the grill and cook.

Monitor the internal temperature of the ham using a probe thermometer.

Cook for about 4 hours (depending on the outside temperature) or until the internal temperature of the ham is at 145°.

Remove from grill, let stand for 5–10 minutes, slice, and serve.

7

FOR HUSBANDS

Here are some ingredients of a good husband.

- *He is pleasant.* Nobody likes an arrogant man. Be pleasant to everyone around you, including your wife, friends, and family. Be warm, kind, positive, understanding, and friendly. It is often said that what we give is what we get back. Try to arrive home as cheery and lighthearted as you can, even after a bad day at the office or when physically exhausted from driving in a traffic jam. Just because your wife may not go out to work does not mean that her work is less strenuous. She might have been struggling with the children and the housework all day.

- *He respects his marriage vows.* Faithfulness is one of the prime qualities a wife wants in her man. Have a sense of loyalty, honor, and duty. Remember that when you were married, you and your wife exchanged sacred vows. The honorable thing is to fulfill the duty to your wife that you took on the day you married.

- *He provides for his family.* Never expect your wife to contribute to the smooth operation of the household. Even in this day and age of women in the workplace, most prefer it as an option rather than a necessary part of their lives. Motherhood and caring for a husband and home usually take priority for her. Never assume that the money you earn is yours to do with as you like. You have a family to think about now and their needs must always come before your own.

- *He is reliable, responsible, and supportive.* Every woman wants her partner to be reliable and there for her when she needs him. Support your wife in all stages of life. Provide reassurance when she is feeling down. Do not belittle her or hurt her ego. If she is working outside the home, understand her work pressures and problems. Be proud of her accomplishments and do not forget to compliment her. Be available when she needs a shoulder to cry on. Let her know that you care for her. When you are not near her, at least make a phone call even if you talk for only a minute or two. After work and on weekends, do things with her or help her in whatever way possible. Even if you are not much help, she will appreciate that you tried. Be a friend to her. When you don't agree with her views, respectfully give your reasons.

- *He is adaptable and sensitive.* As years pass, the glowing woman you fell in love with will not look the same or behave in the same manner. She may be tied up with the pressures at home, like the needs of children or financial obligations. Allow her time to relax by taking some work off her shoulders. Take time together relaxing. Be sensitive to the needs of your wife and look to meet them. Do not let your feelings toward life's changes affect feelings toward your wife. An ideal husband is sensitive to his wife's needs, treats her as an equal, understands when she needs to work late, and helps with housework.

- *He shows respect.* If you expect respect from others, you need to treat them with respect. Respect is reflected in the way one talks and behaves. Always speak in a loving manner and refrain from speaking harshly. A good husband never chooses to belittle, strike, humiliate, or otherwise harm his wife in private or in public. It is better to think before speaking, as it is not possible to take the words back once they have been spoken. Treat her with respect in front of others and at home. Do not look at other women in front of her. Take her opinion into consideration when making important decisions of the family. If you are bringing your buddies home, let her know in advance.

- *He avoids judging and exhibiting emotional baggage.* Many of us have emotional baggage. Do not bring it into the marriage. Many men praise previous wives, girlfriends, or their mother in front of their wives. Avoid judging every action or opinion of your wife's. Understand that she is different from you. Her likes and experiences are different too. Comparing her to other women and implying that she does not measure up can ruin your marriage.

- *He communicates honestly and with integrity.* Communication is the key to a solid marriage. A wife expects honesty in her husband. Honesty builds trust in your relationship. She may forgive your mistakes if you are honest with her and promise not to do it again. Women like men to be open at all times. Do not keep your wife in the dark about what is going on in your life outside the family. Find time to talk with your wife every day, even if it is during dinner time. If you bottle things up and do not share them with your wife, your marriage is in trouble. Be a good listener when she talks. Your wife wants someone to listen and empathize with what's going on in her life. Listen avidly to your wife's complaints. Understand her moods, attitudes, feelings, values, likes, and dislikes. This encourages her to open up to you. And don't keep secrets. Good communication builds trust and strengthens your relationship. Make your wife laugh often. Women love men who are witty and have a sense of humor. When arguments or problems occur, do not let others know about them. Resolve it between the two of you. And when it is resolved, move on and do not rehash it or continue reminding her of her faults. Do not resort to name-calling, hitting, spitting, breaking dishes, or anything else when you lose your temper.

- *He shows love and affection.* As often as you can, show your wife love and affection, and not just to get to bed. Your wife is going to notice and think it's insincere. A good husband appreciates his wife and will notice her even after twenty or fifty years of marriage. She needs you to notice when she wears a new hair style or dresses in something sexy for you. If you fail to notice too many times, she may count it as pointless and quit. Surprise her with something fancy when she least expects it: a trip, a nice dinner, her favorite flowers, or taking her shopping. Most women like to be pampered. Don't forget the special days in her life, like her birthday and your anniversary. Make an effort to initiate spontaneous affection with your wife. Build companionship by doing things together, whether it is a common interest or a hobby. Give her a hug or surprise kiss and tell her how much you love her. Hold hands with her when you're out together. These small gestures help reinforce your commitment to your wife.

- *He protects his wife.* A good husband fends off harm so that his wife feels safe and secure. You hope she feels that when she is with you, no one can harm her. You don't need to be a muscle man, but at least when you are with her, others should not be making a pass at her. Your wife wants you to treat her like a lady when she is with you.

- *He gives her space.* As a husband, you need to understand that your wife cares about other people besides you. She may have parents, relatives, friends, and colleagues who are also part of her life. She may have hobbies, activities, or causes that she is passionate about and involved in. Don't expect her undivided attention. Don't try to stop her if she wants to spend time with friends, relatives, or activities.

In short, if you don't like how you partner treats you, take a minute to notice how you treat your partner and correct your behavior. If you are an ideal husband, that will help your wife to be an ideal wife. A wife usually responds to the way she is treated. If she is treated like she is worthless, she will be worthless to you. If you treat her well, she will be a jewel in your crown, a pleasure to you, and forever a blessing.

Cooking by Faith, Not by Sight

Try this exercise: Stand up, close your eyes, and take ten steps. Can you imagine what it is like to be blind? After just a couple of steps you will probably be disoriented. It is so unnatural for us to walk without looking where we are going, yet this is precisely how we must live in order to obtain true happiness. We must walk by faith, not by sight.

Every decision you make is a either step of faith or a step based on sight. All your decisions work together to determine who you are. They reflect your views of life, yourself, your manhood, and the future.

Will you live a life of faith and virtue, walking by that faith? Or will you live a life based only on what you see and feel, dependent on your own resources, figuring out how to work things to your own advantage?

To our eyes, a life of faith seems a lot riskier. To walk by sight seems to make more sense. However, these two lifestyles are very different and have different outcomes, as the following chart shows:

	Walking by Sight	Walking by Faith
What guides you?	Your senses, eyes, ears, and emotions. External appearances are deceiving. If it feels good, do it.	Virtue and piercing the veil of fear to look behind the curtain and see what's in your soul.
Your outlook on life?	Short term, temporal, no tomorrow, no soul.	Long term, eternal, taking great care with the condition of your soul.
Relationships?	It's all about me; I come to be served.	It's not about me; I come to serve.
Money and possessions?	Must accumulate as much as possible; constant anxiety over money.	Thankful for what you have; sharing with others; all that is not given is lost.
Suffering and inequality?	Whine for justice and equality; deal with suffering by despairing; no hope.	View current afflictions as temporary and character building; justice comes in the long run. Hope.

There are many risks and dangers in the walk of faith. It requires discipline and self-control. There will be pain and suffering. But in the long run, those who walk by faith are rewarded.

Those who walk by sight may appear powerful, successful, and happy. But they usually discover that earthly riches are temporary and ultimately unsatisfying. They should have been more concerned about investing in the condition of their soul for eternity.

We are all challenged to "walk by faith, not by sight." It is as unnatural as walking with our eyes closed. But the more steps we take, the more comfortable this walk will become, and the more confident we will be of the destination of our walk. And ultimately that is what the reward of faith is all about—"to see what we believe."

Moments of Truth in a Recipe

In the kitchen, a "moment of truth" is an instance of adding an ingredient or starting a process that gives the product an opportunity to form (or change) into that perfect recipe.

We all have dozens of "moments of truth" in our own lives every day. They happen when we make a decision regarding our behavior or interactions with others. They shape our life and determine our future. Quite often we pass over these redemptive moments unaware of them. We are too busy to notice. It takes a special focus to become aware of these moments. Often we feel bad when our conscience whispered to us to take a particular action and we ignored it. We usually wish we had acted on what our heart was telling us to do.

An important question to ask is, What motivates the decisions I make at these moments of truth? What is the guiding force behind my decisions? It could one of the following:

- Individualism: What's in it for me?
- Hedonism: If it feels good, do it!
- Minimalism: I'm going to do just enough to get by.
- Relativism: There is no "truth," so anything goes.
- Materialism: Whoever dies with the most toys wins, so I gotta get some!

Or is there something behind your decisions that is more worthy and virtuous? Is there a philosophy out there that leads to a better life?

The most difficult thing can be to act boldly and courageously at the moment of truth. Many of us have good values, and our conscience tells us "what to do." But we often lack the courage to do it, too afraid of what others will think.

So what can we do? Be more attentive to the little or big moments of truth we encounter every day, and then act on them boldly and courageously, without counting the cost or worrying what others will think of us.

The Passion of Cooking

The creative force behind all great art, drama, music, architecture, and writing is passion. Nothing great is accomplished or sustained without it. Passion is what energizes life and makes the impossible possible. Passion gives you a reason to get up in the morning and say, "I'm going to do something with my life today." Without passion, life becomes boring, monotonous, routine, and dull. You were created with the emotions to have passion in your life. Passion is what causes scientists to spend late night hours trying to find the cure to a dreaded disease. Passion takes a good athlete and turns him or her into a great athlete.

A major cause for losing passion is engaging in enterprises that do not use our talents. Each of us has been given specific talents and abilities that are meant to be used in the service of others. You have a special role in this world, and you are supposed to be using your talents to make a contribution with your life. If you don't use your talents you are going to lose your passion. You were not given your special abilities just to sit on them. In fact, it's more like "use it or lose it." Have you ever had that feeling coming home after a long day's work? Rather than feeling satisfied, you feel like you just had the life force sucked from your body?

If you are stuck in a job that does not use your talents to any degree, you are inevitably going to lose your zeal and zest and passion in life. It's going to burn you out. A 2013 Gallup Poll showed that 70 percent of Americans are in a job that they feel does not use their talents.[7] That's tragic. We were designed to use our talents to earn our livelihood, but many of us don't. No wonder people become depressed about their jobs. A lot of people are stuck in a job they hate, where they are not using their talents. They lose their zest for life.

The solution is to live a life that is more than your job. Use your talents with your family, serving others, volunteering, starting a business on the side, coaching, pursuing a hobby, or working in a ministry. No job could possibly use all the talents with which you have been blessed. So you need an outlet that expresses what you are good at.

To fully practice the virtue of enterprise is to use your talents earning your livelihood and serving others with what remains in your "talent tank." Use it or lose it.

8

FISH

When it comes to buying fish and seafood, freshness should never be in doubt. While it's nearly impossible to gauge freshness when you order seafood in a restaurant, you do have control when you're shopping for yourself. Here's what to look for:

- *It should not look dry or have scales coming away.*
- *Everything should have a wet look to it.*
- *The eyes should be clear and the gills should be a vivid red.*
- *The flesh should spring back when touched.*
- *Filets should have an even tone in color and not have any dark or dry spots.*
- *Shop for fish in a place where there is a high turnover of product and lots of activity.*
- *Make sure your fish is nestled in crushed ice. Take a peek around and check whether the surrounding area is clean.*
- *Note the smell. A fishy smell indicates that you need to walk away. A faint salty or seaweed aroma is perfectly acceptable.*

Shrimp should have a shiny, wet appearance with tight scales and, as with all other fish, no odor. Buy shrimp that have been deveined, sometimes referred to as EZ peel.

The basic rule is to cook fish 8 minutes per inch of thickness, or 10 minutes per inch if it's a whole fish. Check it 2 minutes before you think it should be done, keeping in mind that everything keeps cooking for a few minutes after it leaves the grill. Fish is best when it just starts to flake off with a fork.

Grilled Teriyaki Salmon

Ingredients:

One whole salmon fillet, skin-on, pin bones removed

Morton's Sugar Cure

Marinade ingredients:

1 cup soy sauce (use gluten-free soy sauce if cooking gluten-free)

1-inch nob of fresh ginger root, grated

4 to 5 cloves garlic, crushed

2 to 4 tablespoons brown sugar

Preparation:

Combine marinade ingredients in a bowl.

Rub meat side of the filet lightly with Morton's Sugar Cure.

Place marinade ingredients in a large casserole dish or on a plate with sides so the marinade doesn't run.

Place the salmon fillet in the marinade; position so the meat is covered.

Marinate for 1 to 2 hours chilled in the refrigerator.

Remove fillets from marinade and discard marinade.

Fire the grill and set on high (375°).[4*]

4* All temperatures are Fahrenheit.

Method:

Place fillet on grill, skin side down.

Cook until the meat starts to bubble and white juice rises to surface, usually 20 minutes.

Carefully remove from the grill with a spatula and serve.

Smoked Salmon

Ingredients:

1 cup Morton's Sugar Cure

1/2 cup sugar

1/2 cup dark brown sugar

1 tablespoon crushed black peppercorns

2 large salmon fillets, pin bones removed

Preparation:

In a bowl, mix together Morton's Sugar Cure, sugar, brown sugar, and peppercorns.

Spread extra-wide aluminum foil a little longer than the length of the fish and top with an equally long layer of plastic wrap. Sprinkle 1/3 of the rub onto the plastic. Lay 1 side of the fish skin down onto the rub. Sprinkle 1/3 of the rub onto the flesh of the salmon. Place second side of salmon, flesh down onto the first side. Use the remaining rub to cover the skin on the top piece. Fold plastic over to cover then close edges of foil together and crimp tightly around the fish.

Place wrapped fish onto a plank or sheet pan and top with another plank or pan. Weigh with a heavy phone book or a brick or two and refrigerate for 12 hours. Flip the fish over and refrigerate another

12 hours. Some juice will leak out during the process so make sure there's a place for the runoff to gather.

Unwrap fish and rinse off the spices with cold water. Pat salmon with paper towels then place in a cool, dry place (not the refrigerator) until the surface of the fish is dry and matte-like, 1 to 3 hours depending on humidity. A fan may be used to speed the process.

Method:

Fire your grill and set on smoke, 170° to 190°.

Smoke the fish until the thickest part of the fish registers 150°.

Serve immediately or cool to room temperature, wrap tightly, and refrigerate for up to 3 days.

Fish Tacos

Ingredients:

1 pound firm white fish, such as tilapia, snapper, cod, mahimahi, or catfish

2 medium limes, halved

1 medium garlic clove, finely chopped

1/4 teaspoon ground cumin

1/4 teaspoon chili powder

2 tablespoons vegetable oil, plus more for oiling the grill grates

Kosher salt

Freshly ground black pepper

1/2 small head of green or red cabbage (about 14 ounces), cored and thinly sliced

1/2 medium red onion, thinly sliced

1/4 cup coarsely chopped fresh cilantro

6 to 8 soft (6-inch) corn tortillas

Salsa

Sour cream

Hot sauce

Preparation:

Place the fish in a baking dish and squeeze a lime half over it. Add the garlic, cumin, chili powder, and 1 tablespoon of the oil. Season with salt and pepper and turn the fish in the marinade until evenly coated. Refrigerate and let marinate at least 15 minutes. Meanwhile, make the slaw and warm the tortillas.

Combine the cabbage, onion, and cilantro in a large bowl and squeeze a lime half over it. Drizzle with the remaining 1 tablespoon oil, season with salt and pepper, and toss to combine. Taste and add more salt and pepper if necessary; set aside.

Method:

Fire your grill and set at 300°.

Warm the tortillas on the grill flipping to warm both sides, about 5 minutes total. Wrap the warm tortillas in a clean dishcloth and set aside while you prepare the fish.

Remove the fish from the marinade and place on the grill.

Cook without moving until the underside of the fish has grill marks and is white and opaque on the bottom, about 5 minutes. Flip and grill the other side until white and opaque, about another 5 minutes more. Transfer the fish to a plate.

Taste the slaw again and season as needed with more lime juice.

To construct a taco, break up some of the cooked fish, place it in a warm tortilla, and top it with slaw, salsa, sour cream, and hot sauce.

9

FOR SONS

Being a virtuous son requires a great sense of responsibility, spending quality time away from your personal needs, and justly balancing important issues between yourself and your parents. Do you want to know how to be a more manly son?

- Set a goal. What attributes do you want to make you a better son? Focus on those that need improvement to provide a better life for your parents. Set a goal and see it through. Do not allow yourself to be distracted by friends or selfish personal needs.

- Spend time with your parents. A little time spent with your parents can often help achieve a better understanding of one another. Make time to be involved in issues that need attention and your time.

- Sacrifice something for them and ask nothing in return. Parents are our strength. To sacrifice something for them is the best thing a son can do. It will bring them great joy and make you feel wanted and needed as well.

- Show your parents that you care. Always be with them through their happiness and distress. Give them a lot of care, as they wish that from you. Your presence is important.

- Learn something from them. A parent is always willing to lend experience to a son. Try to learn a lot from them. We are always our father's son.

- Perform well in school. If you perform well in school your parents will be happy and reward you for being a great student. This will give them great comfort in knowing their investment in you was not wasted.
- Be an obedient son. Obey your parents' instructions. Your parents have lived longer than you and as a result, their talk comes out of their years of experience.
- Make them proud. Every parent feels pride and grace when a child achieves something in life. Update your parents about every school and work promotion.
- Live up to their expectations. Parents expect their son to avoid evil and to support their values. So make sure you cultivate and nurture your values.
- Try to be understanding. Try to see things from their point of view instead of your own. Give them credit for the wisdom they have acquired from their own experience.
- Always seek your parents' advice. In situations where you have to make big decisions, your parents' advice will help you a lot.
- Be loving. Give you parents boundless love. Treat all their griefs and diseases with the best medicine available, your love.
- Always keep your parents happy. Try to do whatever makes your parents happy. You can make them feel proud by doing fun things with them.

No Self-Contemplation, No Great Recipes

I see it in so many kitchens nowadays: We have become so busy and distracted with the technological economic self-centered postmodern pace of today's culture that we have no time for self-contemplation. Self-contemplation is quietly sitting every day and reviewing questions like:

- Who am I ?
- What is my story?

- Where did I come from?
- Where have I been?
- Where am I going?
- Why am I here?

When we don't take time for self-contemplation, we are not in touch with our personal narrative, our own story. Without that, we are lost. We don't know where to go or what to choose, and without this game plan, we can end up going the wrong way and making the wrong choices.

Our soul is revealed through the unfolding of the story of your personal pilgrimage through this strange land and these strange times. The story that we create about ourselves and our manliness can be fact or fiction.

Some men maintain a fictional story for many years. Soon they buy into that fictional story and sell it to others, hiding the skeletons in their closet and creating elaborate lies to keep them there. Some spend all their time in nostalgia or escapism stories. Many love the drama and imagery of the fictional story about themselves. They believe they are someone they are not. These fictional chapters in a man's life usually cause pain for both the storyteller and those closest to him. These fictional self-stories always come to an end, and that's when the pain sets in. More often than not, it happens at a crossroads during life crisis (health, financial, job, marital) that is a personal moment of truth, sometimes known as the infamous midlife crisis.

When our personal narrative is fact rather than fiction, we suffer less, handle life's bumps better, and generally enjoy life more. To create a factual personal narrative, we should be constantly questioning, reviewing, and challenging our story to make sure it is real. Through self-contemplation, we come to grips with both the vice and virtue in our lives and hold ourselves morally responsible for what we really are. We need to wake up and face both the ugly and beautiful truths of our lives. Only then we can begin to forgive ourselves, work to incorporate humanizing restraints on ourselves, and create a more honest personal narrative. Only then can we be the man we profess to be.

Pursuing a factual personal story happens with continual self-contemplation and examination. In our own minds, we need to speak the unspeakable and force ourselves to hear what we would prefer not to hear: the truth. Without this, we can spend our lifetime living a lie.

The 20 Needs of Young Chefs

- Food (and lots of it!)
- A place of refuge, where they can be safe
- Some discipline and structure in their life
- To play and have fun
- To learn to work with others
- To overcome weaknesses
- To actively participate in events
- To support a superior
- To master a body of knowledge
- To receive help
- To overcome adversity
- To be aggressive
- To dispose of an inferior
- To accomplish something difficult
- To console another
- Some freedom and autonomy in their life
- To control and dominate someone
- To impress others
- To accept blame
- To explore their emotions

Hopeful Cooking

They say that the eyes are the window to the soul. What do you see when you look into the eyes of a young man? I bet a lot of people see fear and hopelessness. It is sad and discouraging, but it is our job as adults to help these young people replace that fear and hopelessness with hope. It is our mission to mentor their souls to hope. In order to give them hope, our own "Hope Cup" must be overflowing. Here are some strategies that can help fill us and others with hope:

1. Lose the "self-image" of failure. Discipline your mind to let go of the self-image of a failure. Stop thinking of yourself as not good at something and you'll lay the foundation for excellence.

2. Stop pointing fingers elsewhere. Take responsibility for your own happiness and stop blaming problems and failures on circumstances or other people.

3. Eliminate the doubt that says, "I can't." Self-doubt is responsible for procrastination, a lack of goals, and quitting before success.

4. Remove positive attraction to unsupportive tasks, people, and places. The lure of unsupportive people, places, and activities (inactivity, too) that keep you from having hope is strong. You must discipline yourself to steer away from these hopeless people, places, and behaviors such as drugs, alcohol, porn, laziness, gluttony, too much TV, and video games.

5. Remove negative feelings about supportive tasks, people, and places. Retrain your mind to enjoy more virtuous hope-filled activities. Tell yourself they are good for you, and then take the medicine. Commit to studying, reading, preparing for tests, completing homework, writing papers, exercising, cleaning up after yourself, and serving others.

6. Rise above worry. Resist focusing on what's not perfect or what could go wrong. Focusing on fearful thoughts

concerning things related to your day can lead to procrastination, nagging, arguments, unhappiness, rage, jealousy,
and being obsessive.

7. Stop feeling overwhelmed with the task at hand. Stop blow-
ing up the "size" and difficulty of routine tasks and decisions
related to reaching your goal. Always try to see them as
manageable.

8. Handle mistakes, setbacks, and delays with patience and
confidence. You cannot plan for unforeseen mistakes, setbacks, and delays. But keep them in perspective. They show
you what you are made of. How you respond to adversity
will predict your future.

Hope is the food of the soul. A soul without hope will wither
and perish. There are many souls that are starving to death for a
lack of hope. Just like the body dies from a lack of nourishment, so a
soul dies when its source of life is gone. That source is hope. Hope's
life-giving work in the soul gives a man reason to get out of bed in
the morning, go to work or school, serve others, live, and lay down
your life for others.

How to Be a Chef of Integrity

You are a chef of integrity to the degree when you live a life consistent with the values that you espouse. Integrity locks in your values
and causes you to live by them. A person of integrity practices what
he or she preaches.

Here are questions to ask when judging your integrity:

- Are you honest with yourself? Are you living consistently
  with your own values and virtues?

- Are the behaviors in which you engage on a daily basis consistent with your values? How do you handle life's unexpected

ups and downs? What you say and do shows the kind of person that lies behind your worldly mask.

- Your integrity shows itself in your work. Do you strive to do the best you can at your work, whether at a job, studies, or homework? A man of true integrity realizes that everything is a statement about who he really is. Your actions speak so loudly that people can no longer hear your words.

- Do you know what you stand for? What you stand for—and what you don't stand for—tells you and the world what kind of person you are.

- What are the five most important values in life? For what would you pay, sacrifice, suffer, or even die? For what would you stand up or refuse to lie down? What do you treasure? What makes you get out of bed every morning? What drives you? What is the guiding and motivating force in your life? The answers to these questions form the foundations of your character. Whenever you are forced to choose between acting on one value over another, choose the one highest on your own personal hierarchy.

- Are you consistent? Can people rely on you or are you a flake? How devoted are you to keeping your word? Can you always be trusted to do the right thing?

- In what kind of shape is your reputation? Do you guard it? Can you fix it? For what do you have a reputation?

- Do you associate with people of integrity? Do you surround yourself with people of character? Birds of a feather flock together.

- What kind of communication do you have with your inner voice? Do you know the difference between the whispers in your ear from the "angel" on your right shoulder, and the "devil" on your left?

- Are your relationships with family and friends completely honest, or are you living a lie? When you are doing and saying one thing on the outside but feeling and believing something different on the inside, it makes life miserable. Open up and spill the beans. Everyone will benefit from your honesty.

Remember that it is easy to make promises but hard to keep them. If you keep promises, every act of integrity makes your character a little stronger. As you improve the quality and strength of your character, all other parts of your life improve also. In no time at all, your family, friends, teammates, teachers, and coworkers will see and appreciate the difference in your relationships with them.

40 Developmental Ingredients for Adolescents

The Search Institute, a Minneapolis nonprofit that researches the developmental needs of adolescents, has identified what it calls 40 Developmental Assets that help young people grow up healthy, caring, and responsible. Every young man and his parents, teachers, coaches, and other adults who care about him should review this list and work to supplement any deficiencies.

1. *Family support.* Family life provides high levels of love and support.
2. *Positive family communication.* A young man and his parent(s) communicate positively, and he seeks advice and counsel from parents.
3. *Other adult relationships.* The young man receives support from three or more nonparent adults.
4. *Caring neighborhood.* The young person experiences caring neighbors.

5. *Caring school climate.* School provides a caring, encouraging environment.

6. *Parental involvement in schooling.* Parent(s) are actively involved in helping the young man succeed in school.

7. *Community values youth.* The young man perceives that adults in the community value him.

8. *Youth as resources.* The young man is given a useful role in the community.

9. *Service to others.* The young man serves in the community one hour or more per week.

10. *Safety.* The young man feels safe at home, school, and in the neighborhood.

11. *Family boundaries.* The young man's family has clear rules and consequences and monitors his whereabouts.

12. *School boundaries.* The school provides clear rules and consequences.

13. *Neighborhood boundaries.* Neighbors take responsibility for monitoring the young man's behavior.

14. *Adult role models.* Parents and other adults model positive, responsible behavior.

15. *Positive peer influence.* The young man's close friends model responsible behavior.

16. *High expectations.* Parents and teachers encourage the young man to do well.

17. *Creative activities.* The young man spends three or more hours per week in lessons or practice in music, theater, or other arts.

18. *Youth programs.* The young man spends three or more hours per week in sports, clubs, organizations at school, or community organizations.

19. *Religious community.* The young man spends one hour or more per week in activities in a religious institution.

20. *Time at home.* The young man is out with friends "with nothing special to do" two or fewer nights per week.

21. *Achievement motivation.* The young man is motivated to do well in school.

22. *School engagement.* The young man is actively engaged in learning.

23. *Homework.* The young man does at least one hour of homework every school day.

24. *Bonding to school.* The young man cares about his school.

25. *Reading for pleasure.* The young man reads for pleasure three or more hours per week.

26. *Caring.* The young man places high value on helping other people.

27. *Equality and social justice.* The young man places high value on promoting equality and reducing hunger and poverty.

28. *Integrity.* The young man acts on his convictions and stands up for his beliefs.

29. *Honesty.* The young man "tells the truth even when it is not easy."

30. *Responsibility.* The young man accepts and takes personal responsibility.

31. *Restraint.* The young man believes it is important not to be sexually active or to use alcohol or other drugs.

32. *Planning and decision making.* The young man knows how to plan ahead and make choices.

33. *Interpersonal competence.* The young man has empathy, sensitivity, and friendship skills.

34. *Cultural competence.* The young man has knowledge of and comfort with people of different cultural, racial, and ethnic backgrounds.

35. *Resistance skills.* The young man can resist negative peer pressure and dangerous situations.

36. *Peaceful conflict resolution.* The young man seeks to resolve conflict nonviolently.

37. *Personal power.* The young man feels he has control over "things that happen to him."

38. *Self-esteem.* The young man reports having a high self-esteem.

39. *Sense of purpose.* The young man reports that "my life has a purpose."

40. *Positive view of personal future.* The young man is optimistic about his personal future.

10

SIDE DISHES

Barbecue is undoubtedly one of our favorite foods. It makes us proud to be American, and we view summer as a free license to eat as much barbecue as possible. Whether it's tender brisket, fall-off-the-bone ribs, or pulled pork, barbecue can do no wrong. We are to a smoker as moths are to a flame this time of year—we can't get enough and we'll keep coming back for more.

Every leading role needs a supporting one too, and in barbecue's case, the sidekick packs a serious punch. Short ribs look fantastic on their own, but next to a plate of bbq beans and coleslaw, they're a showstopper. And while good barbecued chicken makes us never want to eat chicken any other way, it isn't complete without a pile of potato wedges by its side.

Here are five of my favorite barbecue side dishes that totally steal the show:

Potato Wedges

Ingredients:

5 large russet potatoes, scrubbed and cut lengthwise into 1 1/2-inch wedges

Lawry's Seasoned Salt

Extra-virgin olive oil

Freshly ground pepper

Preparation:

Place potatoes wedges in a plastic bag.

Pour extra-virgin olive oil in the bag.

Sprinkle Lawry's Seasoned Salt and black pepper in the bag.

Shake vigorously.

Method:

Preheat grill to medium-high, about 300°.

Place potato wedges directly on the grill.

Grill about 20 minutes, turning occasionally, until blackened with grill marks and a knife tip pierces through with little resistance.

Serve with Hidden Valley Ranch dressing made with real sour cream.

BBQ Beans

Ingredients:

Three 28-ounce cans baked beans, preferably Bush's Original Baked Beans

1 medium green bell pepper, seeded, deveined, and cut into quarter-inch dice

1 small onion, cut into quarter-inch dice

1/2 cup Worcestershire sauce

1/2 cup packed light-brown sugar

2 tablespoons yellow mustard

1/2 cup finely chopped celery

4 tablespoons ketchup

2 pounds ground beef

Preparation:

Fry ground beef, breaking into small chunks. Drain off grease.

Put beans and remaining ingredients into a large pot.

Mix in ground beef. Stir thoroughly.

Fire grill and set on 275°.

Method:

Grill uncovered for 45 minutes.

Stir, and cook for an additional 30 minutes.

Serve warm.

Pea Salad

Ingredients:

4 slices bacon or bacon substitute

1 16-ounce package frozen green peas

1/2 cup chopped onions

1/2 cup Miracle Whip

One small head of iceberg lettuce. Cut and shred into "1/2-inch by 2-inch" strips

1/2 cup sliced water chestnuts

Preparation:

Combine all ingredients in a large bowl and mix thoroughly.

Method:

Before serving, refrigerate 60 minutes or until chilled.

Cabbage Salad

Ingredients:

1 head green cabbage, cut into bite sized pieces

2 green peppers, thinly sliced

1 red onion, thinly sliced

1 red pepper, thinly sliced

1/4 cup sugar

1/2 cup distilled white vinegar

3 tablespoons mustard seed

2 tablespoons celery seed

1 cup canola oil

Preparation:

Combine all ingredients in container with a lid.

Combine and whisk.

Pour over cabbage.

Method:

Marinate overnight.

Mix again next day and serve cold.

Seafood Salad

Ingredients:

1 can crabmeat

1/2 pound mini shrimp

2 cans minced clams

1 container of premade clam dip

1 small container of small curd cottage cheese

1/4 cup finely sliced green onion

1 teaspoon Traeger Prime Rib Rub

Preparation:

In a large bowl, mix all the ingredients until smooth.

Method:

Before serving, refrigerate 60 minutes or until chilled.

Serve with waved potato chips.

11

FOR FRIENDS

The essence of manly friendship is about care and respect. It has nothing to do with money, or "the cool factor." A true friend is there for you, no matter what, and having such a person in your life is a great gift. Here are ten tools to help you create better friendships:

1. *Forgiveness* is important because everyone makes mistakes. Rather than turning your back on a friend who has hurt you, talk about your pain. If this person is a real friend, he will apologize.

2. *Reliability* is a cornerstone of good friendship. Knowing that you can call on someone who will be there for you and you know has your back is empowering and a great comfort.

3. *If you want to have a friend, learn to be a friend.* Giving what you want to get is the best way to show someone how to be your friend. People generally like us because we like them.

4. *Envy and jealousy will kill a friendship.* Your friend may have everything you think you want, but if you are green with envy, your friend will sense that something's out of sync in your relationship. So count your blessings, which should include having a friend who inspires you to achieve your goals.

5. *Negativity is the antithesis of friendship.* No friendship is going to be perfect all of the time, but keep the bad vibes away; they can only undermine the good thing you've got going.

6. *Deep discussions* are a treasure of friendship. Having a friend who won't judge you can make your life better. Letting out your feelings with a trusted ally is good therapy.

7. *Sharing your feelings and listening to others* are important parts of any good relationship. For some reason, women seem to be better at this than men, so guys, let's be better buddies to each other.

8. Happiness can come from *knowing you have good people in your life.* If you don't have a family of your own, having your friends as family is a true privilege.

9. *Independence* is an important part of good friendships. Your friend, no matter how close he may be, can't be there for you every minute; almost no one can. That would make for an unhealthy dependency; friendship needs to be a two-way street.

10. *Old friends* are reliable and can make us feel a little safer. Someone from your past may be more than just someone you once knew. For many reasons, it's easier to feel close to people you have known for a long time. There is trust there, as well as the knowledge of how someone behaves under a variety of situations.

Walking the Fence of Manhood

The near occasion of vice is the "fence" that divides the Land of Life (virtue) and the Desert of Death (vice). And this is no literary exaggeration.

Most men walk this fence without even knowing it. Some are completely innocent, unawakened by vice. Temptation bites them, they lose their balance, and fall headlong into the Desert of Death. Even the best intended are susceptible because we humans have lost our equilibrium. We all have an inclination toward vice. Because of this, being on that fence is a dangerous place. Many of us have such poor balance that we fall due to our weak wills. Sometimes we even choose to jump in deliberately.

If a meteor comes too close to the earth, it is pulled into the planet's gravity and ultimately destroyed as it burns up in the atmosphere. So too, many men have no intention of succumbing to vice; but by putting themselves near beguiling situations, they are pulled in as the gravity of temptation is too strong to resist.

Men fail, feel remorse, and repent, but then they do nothing to rectify the lifestyle that got them into trouble in the first place. Within no time, they leave the sure paths of virtue and climb back onto the Fence of Temptation, saying to themselves, "I can handle this!" But they are mesmerized by the glamour of vice, lose their balance because of weakness, and fall into the very place they swore they never would go again. Broken and guilt-ridden, they kick themselves in the butt for being so weak.

Men must uproot the near occasions of vice; they simply have to stay further away from the fence. Whether they admit it or not, men retain the inclination for vice. They can even make matters worse by creating the false illusion that they are stronger than they really are. They mistakenly believe that they can approach the fence because they are strong. They are wrong.

Eating-disorder specialists advise their patients to avoid shopping for groceries when hungry and to shop with a list rather than shop compulsively. Likewise, men can take steps to avoid the near occasion of sin and stay off the fence between virtue and vice. If watching TV draws you into sin, leave it off. If you can't leave it off, call the satellite or cable company and cut it off. If you have a problem with pornography or online gambling, move your computer to a visible place. Or if that is no solution, get rid of it. Yes, get rid of the computer.

If you have a group of friends who lead you into sinful activities, then politely leave that group. Don't let yourself be led astray; bad company corrupts good morals.

Walk a different route to work to avoid lustful images. Anticipate inflammatory words from antagonists, and avoid drawing them out. Reduce your credit card limit, or cut up the card altogether. Don't keep alcohol in your house if you can't control drinking. Avoid idle, silly, and risqué conversation. Avoid gossip, including celebrity gossip in entertainment magazines, on radio and on television talk shows. Speak only when necessary—listen more. Order and discipline your day as much as possible to avoid compulsiveness.

Self-Discipline and Sticking to the Recipe

Self-discipline is how we safeguard our souls from harmful things. Keeping "custody of our spirit" enables us to be responsible guardians and keepers of that soul. Custody of our spirit means avoiding not just the vice itself but well-known traps that cause us to fall into vice. It means that we are not fixed on the things of the world and conforming to its vicious ways but on virtue and the path to living a manly life. Let's look at a few less obvious ways that vice threatens our ability to maintain good custody of our spirits.

Lust

Men can't surf the Internet or do just about anything without being assaulted by the vice of lust. It has become socially acceptable, and at younger and younger ages, to sexualize and objectify the body. Men more than women are susceptible to this because there is a stronger chemical response in men that starts with the eyes. In our pornographic culture, how can a man keep from falling into the sin of adultery with his eyes? The answer is very simple. Stop looking. Turn the other way. Even giving undue attention to immodest dress or a sexualized appearance is a snare; it is the slippery slope that leads to wanting more and more. Keeping good custody of our spirit means not letting your eyes wander around the room, not undressing women with your eyes, perusing lewd pictures, and even steering away from TV shows or channels on which you will find indecent images. For some men it means a complete transformation of the mind as to how women are perceived and even how we perceive ourselves.

Materialism

We lose custody of our spirit by always shopping for something better, for the next best thing. In America the vice of materialism and the enticement of new things has reached monstrous proportions, and few are resisting it. The iPad, iPod, iBooks, iPhone—even the names of these gadgets reveal, perhaps unconsciously, our uncontrolled self-absorption: It is all about *I*, not *we* or *us*. Keeping custody of our spirit means acquiring what we *need* rather than what we *want* and not hoarding what we have but sharing it with others, especially the less fortunate.

Pride

The temptation to pride isn't just about desiring fame and fortune. Through technology, it has taken on a more cunning temptation. Social media, while often serving to connect old friends and family, also feeds individualism. With Facebook, Twitter, and dozens of other networking services, people post every thought and action for the world to see, fostering narcissism and self-absorption. When it comes to social networking, many of us need to exercise discipline and great caution to maintain custody of our spirit and avoid vanity. When I post a "tweet" on Twitter or a photo on Facebook, am I flaunting my own ego? Am I just wasting my and other people's time?

Self-discipline and custody of our spirit helps us to walk in the world and keep our hearts unstained by it. As we continually seek what is manly, we can walk in the truths that women are not objects but reflections of our own humanity, that we should use our possessions for our own good and the good of others, and that a meek and gentle heart helps us shun worldly vice and live a virtuous life.

How to Cook More Friendliness

Virtue is the common thread that binds the tapestry of humanity. The easiest way to be friendly to others, especially those you don't like, is to see yourself in them. The secret is to look for and recognize the things that you have in common with others. Most of those things are our shared virtue and humanity. That guy over there loves like you, fears like you, hopes like you, suffers like you, and laughs like you. Seeing yourself in others then gives new meaning to the phrase, "treat others like you would like to be treated."

Here are suggestions for ways to grow in friendliness.

We spend a lot of mental energy evaluating other people, judging their actions, considering their faults and merits, comparing ourselves to them, envying them, being bothered by them, and so on. It's easy to start focusing on people's faults and to allow that to dominate our relationships with them. But if you think about it, the faults we find in others are usually small annoyances or irritations that we have inflated to colossal proportions. What if we spent less time worrying about others' faults and more time improving our relationships with them?

Cultivate friendships and happiness toward those who are happier than we are. When we meet people who are consistently happy and content, we should seek out their friendship. We can learn from them and share in their joy. Often we experience envy when we meet such people; we can become so busy wishing we were happy that we lose the opportunity to share and learn from them. Sometimes we might be so displeased about someone's happiness that we become determined to squelch it entirely. We should share other people's happiness.

On the flip side, we can also grow in friendliness by having compassion for those who are unhappy. When we are suffering, we are grateful to others who offer support, even a friendly smile or a knowing glance. If the person who is unhappy is not someone you know or like, and finding the compassion to reach out can be a great act of friendliness. Also, when you are suffering, thinking of others who are feeling the same way and feeling compassion for them can help lift you out of your dungeon of self-pity.

These suggestions for growth in friendliness call on us to look for commonality and connection with others, rather than using envy, judgment, and hatred to distance ourselves from people. In the end, friendliness has a simple formula: judge less, love more.

CONCLUSION

THE END-ALL RECIPE FOR VIRTUOUS MANHOOD

A young man once asked me for a recipe for virtuous manhood. Unfortunately, he did not grow up with a model of a man to follow. So I have been thinking about the ingredients of virtuous manhood, as well as things that can ruin the whole pie, and that is what inspired me to write this book.

So what is that end-all recipe for virtuous manhood?

1. *Be a pursuing disciple of virtue.* It all starts here. Virtue has to have a man's heart and passion before he can be a virtuous husband or father. Everything else comes from this focus on virtue. If this focus is authentic, it will reflect in our heart. Be a worshiper and learner of virtue! Leave no question about the guiding and motivating force of your life. Your wife will be able to follow your lead when you are following virtue. Your kids will respect you when you are following virtue. (On the flip side, if you are not true to virtue, your family will see through it and despise any hypocrisy.)

2. *Humility.* To be virtuous means we have to lay down the pride that wants to be right. We must realize that we all make mistakes, we are all human, and we have corrupted thinking that needs to be refocused by virtue. Until a man comes to the place where he realizes his biggest enemy is his pride, he cannot be a truly virtuous man.

3. *A good mentor.* A mentor is another man whom you trust, who is mature, and has been serving virtue longer and knows where the pitfalls are. If we compare this to a race or journey, this is the person ahead of you whom you can follow. This story illustrates:

The Man in the Golden Shorts

by Mark Hamill

There once was a man who liked to run . . . occasionally. He had a neighbor who loved to run . . . all the time. He was a fanatic. One day "fanatic man" invited "occasional man" to join him for an upcoming 10-K "fun run" (talk about an oxymoron). Without bothering to do the math—that 10-K equals 6.5 miles—occasional man agreed. And so it happened early one Saturday, occasional man and fanatic man found themselves registering for the Moreland Days 10-K, along with 100 other jogger-nauts.

Everyone got numbers pinned to their shirts and a map of the route.

The atmosphere among the participants was festive, and camaraderie continued even after the starter's pistol cracked the new day. Occasional man got caught up in all the excitement and lost his map. No matter; he would just stick by the fanatic man . . . whatever it took.

This was a good plan—for the first mile. But the knot of racers soon stretched into a snake, with the fittest athletes forming the head and the spent ones streaming behind.

Fanatic man moved effortlessly to the snout of the beast, leaving occasional man lost in the bowels. This bothered occasional man, but his mind soon turned to more pressing matters—survival. The second mile had passed under foot and somewhere in the middle of the third, a thought began worrying the edges of his consciousness. He might not make it to the finish line, in fact, he could actually die out here.

A mile later the panic in his brain burned off like the morning fog and the future became clear. The issue wasn't really if he would die, but when.

Meanwhile, the serpent slithered its way through quiet neighborhoods around a golf course and into a nearby forest preserve. Occasional man was all alone now. He could see only one other runner—a man in golden shorts about 20 yards ahead. Occasional man prayed the stranger still had his map and knew where he was going. This was very important because occasional man knew if he got too far off course the police wouldn't be able to find his body.

The man in gold pulled occasional man along as if they were short-roped together. When he zigged, occasional man zigged; when he zagged, occasional man zagged, step by painful step through mile five into mile six. Finally they reached Main Street with its Frappuccino-sipping spectators.

Having made it back to civilization occasional man thought about collapsing, but his pride wouldn't allow it. Dying alone in agony was one thing; spilling your guts in front of strangers was quite another. He finished the race and collapsed into the warm congratulations of well-wishers—including fanatic man, who looked like he just got back from walking the dog.

Occasional man gave his neighbor a bear hug, soaking him with sweat. Later that night he would duct-tape the doors and windows of fanatic man's house shut and put a for sale sign in his yard. But right now he had more pressing business and went to find the man in the golden shorts. When he saw the exhausted stranger, leaning against a tree, occasional man approached him and said, "Thanks. You saved my life."

The moral of this racy tale? Quite simple—really: "Better a role model in sight than a hero over the hill."

At times we find ourselves in unfamiliar territory, afraid of stopping, and unsure about proceeding. We search frantically for anyone who knows where he or she is going—someone whose footsteps we can follow because we can literally step in them.

Heroes inspire us by their exploits, yet they are so far ahead of us we seldom see them in the flesh. And while we are told to "fix our eyes on virtue," we also need our role models in the same heat as us.

As you run life's marathon, whose tail are you following: a father's, friend's, a big sister's, teacher's, grandparent's, or pastor's? Have you looked that person in the eye lately and said, "Thanks. You saved my life"? And on the other side of the race, who's following you? What are you waiting for?

4. *A healthy peer structure.* If a man can't let go of old friends, they will hold him back and keep his attention divided. "Bad company corrupts good character."

5. *A younger man to invest in and mentor.* This is the man who is following you as you follow virtue. It can be your son, but there needs to be someone in front you and someone behind you.

6. *Integrity in the big three vices.* After pride, money, sex, and power are a man's three biggest pitfalls. The love of money will ruin the heart of man, and it is the cause of all kinds of evil. One does not have to have money to love it. Sex, porn, and lust will ruin the marriage of a man faster than anything else. Power and control will ruin the effectiveness of money. The virtuous man must let virtue guide his path.

7. *A mission that costs something, whether time, effort, energy, or money.* You need a mission that you believe in enough to willingly sacrifice for it.

8. *A passion for virtue at home.* The man is to be the leader of the home. This means he gathers his wife and kids and they

talk about virtue. He makes sure that the tone of the home is based on virtue.

9. *A working list of priorities.* For example:

- Faith
- Family
- Financial needs of the family
- Friends
- Football

A "working list" means that we need to tackle these in the right order. Football does not come before my family. Friends do not come before my faith.

1. *An open life.* There should be nothing to hide in your schedule, on your computer, with your finances, or anything else. Be completely honest with yourself, your spouse, and others. There is no room for lying.

2. *A cheek that can turn.* You have to be able to turn the other cheek

3. *A heart that does not give up easily.* It is also called going the extra mile

4. *Care for the widow, orphan, and the poor.* Do you have to? No, but it makes a man great. He doesn't have to care for the less fortunate, but he does anyway.

5. *Fight off the urge to judge and impute motives of others.* Wise men do not jump to conclusions about others. Fools think they know what drives others when they have not asked.

6. Have a *thankful heart and attitude.*

7. Finally, a *eulogy focus.* Get up every day and try to work on the one phrase that people will write on your tombstone when you have departed. When you are gone, no one will care what your resume looks like.

ENDNOTES

1. Claudia Puig, "Youths in Poll Say TV Is Harmful Influence," *Los Angeles Times*, February 27, 1995, http://articles.latimes.com/1995-02-27/news/mn-36683_1_antisocial-behavior.
2. Proverbs 3:14.
3. Proverbs 8:11.
4. Proverbs 3:16–18.
5. Isaiah 42:3; Matthew 12:20.
6. http://govleaders.org/quotes-leaders.htm
7. Beth Stebner, "Workplace Morale Heads Down," *New York Daily News*, June 24, 2013, www.nydailynews.com/news/national/70-u-s-workers-hate-job-poll-article-1.1381297.